INVISIBLE
INFLUENCE

The Hidden Forces
That Shape Behavior

Jonah Berger

Simon & Schuster Paperbacks

New York   London   Toronto   Sydney   New Delhi

To Jordan and Zoë

———

Simon & Schuster Paperbacks
An Imprint of Simon & Schuster, Inc.
1230 Avenue of the Americas
New York, NY 10020

Names and identifying characteristics of students, study participants,
and others have been changed.

First Simon & Schuster trade paperback edition June 2017

SIMON & SCHUSTER PAPERBACKS and colophon are registered
trademarks of Simon & Schuster, Inc.

For information about special discounts for bulk purchases,
please contact Simon & Schuster Special Sales at 1-866-506-1949
or business@simonandschuster.com.

The Simon & Schuster Speakers Bureau can bring authors to
your live event. For more information or to book an event contact
the Simon & Schuster Speakers Bureau at 1-866-248-3049 or visit
our website at www.simonspeakers.com.

Manufactured in the United States of America

10 9 8 7 6 5 4 3 2

ISBN 978-1-4767-5969-2
ISBN 978-1-4767-5973-9 (pbk)
ISBN 978-1-4767-5975-3 (ebook)

Praise for

INVISIBLE

INFLUENCE

"With great insight, Jonah Berger removes the cloak of invisibility from powerful sources of influence and resolves fascinating mysteries of human behavior."

—Robert Cialdini, author of *Influence* and *Pre-Suasion*

"If you want to know what really influences your behavior, read Jonah Berger's latest eye-opening book, packed with thought-provoking research, memorable stories, and powerful insights. A terrific read!"

—William Ury, author of *Getting to Yes with Yourself*

"As he did with *Contagious*, Jonah Berger takes us deep beneath the surface of things, with mesmerizing results. *Invisible Influence* is a book with the power to transform the way we see ourselves and our place in the world."

—Arianna Huffington, author of *Thrive*

"Jonah Berger has done it again: written a fascinating book that brims with ideas and tools for how to think about the world."

—Charles Duhigg, author of *The Power of Habit*

"From the very first page, this book will change the way you look at yourself—and others. Eye-opening and thoroughly engaging."

—Amy Cuddy, author of *Presence*

"Whether you want to influence others, make smarter decisions, or just better understand the mystery that is human behavior, this book will show you how. A terrific, insightful read."

—Tony Hsieh, CEO of Zappos

"Berger offers an engaging guide to the concept of social influence. . . . Berger's prose is consistently entertaining, applying science to real life in surprising ways and explaining research through narrative. . . . His book fascinates because it opens up the moving parts of a mysterious machine, allowing readers to watch them in action."

—*Publishers Weekly*

"Berger picks up where his *Contagious: Why Things Catch On* (2013) left off to explore why we desire what we do—and more, why we act as we do, politically, socially, economically, and emotionally. . . . He does a good job of distilling scientific insights into easily understood object lessons on social psychology."

—*Kirkus Reviews*

"This winding exploration of our collective psyche is fascinating."

—*The Washington Post*

"Jonah continues to be one of the most innovative psychological researchers publishing today. His insights are not only thought-provoking and counterintuitive, he manages to express them in a practical and pragmatic way. I'll read anything he writes—and use it, too."

—Ryan Holiday, author of *Trust Me I'm Lying*
and *Growth Hacker Marketing*

"*Invisible Influence* is that rare business book that's both informative and enough fun to take to the beach."

—Anne Fisher, Fortune.com

"Grab one or both of his books and read them through the lens of your own business. Just maybe you will become more effective at influencing your customers."

—Inc.com

Contents

Introduction

Think about a choice you made recently. Any choice. Which breakfast cereal to buy, movie to see, or place to have lunch. Or even a more important decision: which person to date, political candidate to support, or career to pursue.

Why did you make that choice? Why did you pick the particular option you ended up choosing?

Seems like an easy question. While various idiosyncratic reasons may come to mind, in general, they all point in the same direction: you. *Your* personal tastes and preferences. *Your* likes and dislikes. Which potential mate *you* found funny or attractive. Whether the candidate's policy stance matches *your* own. The notion that our choices are driven by our own personal thoughts and opinions seems so obvious that it is not even worth mentioning.

Except that it's wrong.

Without our realizing it, others have a huge influence on almost every aspect of life.[1] People vote because others are voting, eat more when others are eating, and buy a new car because their neighbors have recently done the same. Social influence affects the products people buy, health plans they choose, grades they get in school, and careers they follow. It shapes whether people save for retirement, invest in the stock market, donate money, join a fraternity, save energy, or adopt new innovations. Social influence even affects whether people engage in criminal activity or are satisfied with their job. Ninety-nine-point-nine percent of all decisions are shaped by others. It's hard to find a decision or behavior that isn't affected by other people.

In fact, looking across all domains of our lives, there is only one place we don't seem to see social influence.

Ourselves.

I started studying the science of social influence—the way others affect our behavior—by biking around Palo Alto, California, looking for BMWs.

Palo Alto is one of the world's most expensive places to live. Stock options and IPOs have fattened the pockets of many residents and have also pushed up everything from housing prices to private school tuition. Ferrari and Maserati have dealerships nearby; lunch at one of the high-end restaurants can run close to $200 per person.

Looking for BMWs was like hunting for Easter eggs. There was no surefire way to know where to find them, so I relied on a little intuition and a lot of luck. I slowly biked up and down different streets, scanning cars for the telltale shape and logo. Then, at each corner, I would stop and try to guess which direction had the best chance of success. Dentist's office to the left? Dentists tend to drive nice cars, so why not do a quick loop of the parking lot. High-end grocery store to the right? Worth a shot.

Every time I found a BMW, I reached into my messenger bag, pulled out a piece of paper, and gingerly tucked it under one of the windshield wipers. These weren't coupons for body shops or advertisements for auto detailing. We weren't selling anything at all.

Instead, Princeton professor Emily Pronin and I were interested in how different factors influenced car buying. Which factors people thought influenced their own car purchase decision and how much those same factors played a role in someone else's BMW purchase.

In addition to standard factors like price, gas mileage, and reliability, the survey also asked about more social influences. Did their friends' opinions affect their decision? What about whether the car was associated with cool or high-status people?[2]

Each respondent answered the set of questions twice: once for themselves, and once for another person they knew who also drove a BMW. How much was that other person's BMW purchase influenced by things like price and gas mileage? Whether cool or high-status people drove something similar?[3]

After biking around in circles most of the day, I had left surveys on more than a hundred BMWs. Each with a self-addressed envelope for people to mail their responses back.

And then, I waited.

The first day the mailman couldn't come fast enough. But when I opened the mailbox, all that was inside was disappointment. Just a bunch of random coupons and a furniture company catalog. No one had returned the survey.

The next day my optimism was tempered with caution. I sauntered by the mailbox and peeked inside. Still nothing. Now I was starting to get worried. Had people ignored the survey? Maybe the envelopes had blown away?

By the third day a feeling of dread accompanied the mail. If there were still no responses, I'd have to go out and find new BMWs (or we'd have to come up with a different approach). But finally, way in the back of the mailbox was the answer I'd been waiting for. One of the small, white envelopes that I had placed on a car windshield a couple days before.

The next day there were a few more responses. And a bunch more the day after that. We were in business. We took the responses and compared people's perceptions of themselves with their perceptions of others. What influenced their BMW purchase versus what influenced someone else's BMW purchase.

Many things were relatively similar. Not surprisingly, people thought factors like price and gas mileage mattered a lot, and they were equally important for both themselves and others. Price had a big impact on their own BMW purchase, and they thought it had a similarly large impact on whether another person had bought a BMW as well.

But when it came to assessing the impact of social influence, things changed. It wasn't that people didn't think social influence mattered. They did. They were keenly aware that car-buying decisions were affected by what friends thought and whether cool or high-status people drove the car. In fact, they readily acknowledged that social influence had a big impact on what cars people buy.

Except when those "people" were themselves.

When they considered someone else's BMW purchase, the effect of social influence was obvious. They could easily recognize that someone's tastes shifted based on what their friends thought or the pressure to fit in.

But when it came to turn that same microscope on their own BMW purchase, *poof!* Social influence vanished. They saw no evidence of it. When they held up a mirror to their own actions, they didn't think social influence had any effect.

And it wasn't just cars. Other situations show the same asymmetry. Whether buying clothes, voting on political issues, or driving courteously, people recognized that social influence had an impact.

Except when it came to them. People could see social influence affecting others' behavior, but not their own.

One possible explanation is social desirability. Maybe people don't think they're influenced by others because being influenced is a bad thing. Society tells us to be ourselves and live above the influence—to avoid being a lemming and going with the herd. If being influenced is bad, maybe people don't think they are swayed because they don't want to see themselves in a negative light.

But it isn't that simple. Even when being influenced was a good thing, people still didn't think it affected them.

It's polite to consider local customs, for example, when visiting a place you don't know well. And when picking out clothes for a formal event, going rogue isn't usually a positive thing. Yet, even in situations like these when it was good to be influenced, people still didn't think they were affected.

Because there is an even more subtle reason we don't think social influence affects us. We can't see it.

ONLY YOU . . .

You just started your junior year of high school, and to celebrate, your parents decide that it's time for you to get a job. You've lived off them long enough, they say, and it's time to make your own spending money. Just a part-time position that will get you out of the house for a few hours a couple times a week. It'll build character and teach you the ways of the world.

Having only babysat and mowed a few lawns, your résumé is not exactly sparkling, but you're able to snag a part-time position bagging groceries at the local supermarket. Not the most exciting job, but it sure beats cleaning out the meat case.

You've just begun to master the ins and outs of paper and plastic when you run into one of your new coworkers in the break room. You've seen her bagging over in lane seven for a couple weeks now and you can't help but notice how pretty she is. She introduces herself and the two of you start talking. About your boss, your respective high schools, and the trick she learned to keep tomatoes from bruising.

Next week you run into her a couple more times. And the week after that a couple more. You talk for even longer. Soon, you find yourself picking shifts based on when you know she'll be there. You start whistling while you work, and eventually, you build up enough courage to ask her out.

And two hundred and seven dinners, ninety-two long walks, three vacations, and one short-lived breakup later, you find yourself getting married to the only person you could ever see yourself spending the rest of your life with.

The idea of a soul mate has existed for thousands of years. In *The Symposium*, Plato wrote that humans originally had four legs, four arms, and a head made of two faces. They could walk equally well backward and forward, and so terrible was their might and strength that they threatened the very gods who were supposed to be ruling over them. Something had to be done.

The gods discussed various solutions. Some wanted to annihilate the human race—wipe them out forever. But one of the gods, Zeus, had a more creative idea. Humans provided gods with various tributes and offerings, so why kill them off entirely? Instead, each human would be split in half. This would teach them a lesson. It would diminish humanity's strength and punish humans for their pride.

And so it went. Each human was divided down the middle. Like a tree trunk cut in two.

Not surprisingly, these split humans were miserable. Even when their wounds healed, they cast about, longing for their other half. Forever searching for the piece that would make them whole.

A lot has changed since Plato's time, but the notion of a one, true love for each of us has remained. Tinder swipes may have supplanted love letters and hooking up may have replaced elaborate courtships, but most people still believe that there is a Mr. or Ms. Right out there, waiting to be found. Like two halves of a circle, or two peas in a pod, someone, somewhere out there will complete you. Your missing puzzle piece, your perfect fit. R&B songs and romantic comedies reinforce this idea again and again. If you've been unlucky in love, don't fret: you just haven't met your soul mate yet.

Scan the wedding section of a newspaper, or ask most married people how they met, and you'll get a similar answer: *From the moment I saw him, I just knew . . . There was a chemistry I'd never felt with anyone else . . . A spark went off and I could tell she was the right one for me . . .*

Most people find any other possibility slightly upsetting. Want to make a happily married friend angry with you? Try suggesting that they might have been equally happy with someone else.

Our partners may not be perfect, but they are ours. And we are 110 percent certain that it couldn't have been anyone else.

We are all princes with a glass slipper, searching for that one and only Cinderella whose foot will fit.

Look at how most Americans meet their future spouse, though, and you'll notice something interesting. There are more than 320 million people in the United States. Drop the married ones and you are left with around 160 million. Prefer one gender more than another and you are left with around 80 million people that could be right for you.

Some of those are the wrong age, support the wrong political party, or—heaven forbid—love polka music; but even once you filter out all of these mismatches, you are left with millions of people. A lot of folks who could potentially be Mr. or Ms. Right.

Do this same exercise with the world population and there are hundreds of millions of people. Any of whom might be your soul mate.

Look at where people end up meeting their future spouse, though, and it's pretty narrowly concentrated. In fact, over a third of Americans meet their husband or wife at one of two places: work or school.[4]

Now, that by itself isn't surprising. People spend a lot of time at work and school, and it's tough to fall in love with someone you never got the chance to meet.

But step back for a moment and consider what that means. Sure, there might be only one right person for each of us. Out of hundreds of millions of people, just one soul mate. But what's the chance that this person just happened to start bagging groceries at the same time we did? Can all of us be that lucky?

Professor Richard Moreland's undergraduate personality psychology course at the University of Pittsburgh was like many courses you might have taken in college. It was held in a large, fan-shaped lecture hall with stadium seating. The space had close to two hundred seats, filled with mostly freshman and sophomores, with a few juniors and seniors mixed in. Around half the students were men, half were women, and there was the usual array of jocks and geeks, slackers and go-getters.

Psychology classes often offer extra credit for participating in academic research, and Professor Moreland's course was no different. At the end of the semester, students were asked if they wanted to complete a short survey. Most said yes.

The survey was simple. Students, both male and female, were shown photos of four women (labeled A, B, C, and D) and asked to answer a few questions about each. How attractive did they find each woman? Did they think they would enjoy spending time with her? Would they like to become friends with her?

None of the four women were particularly distinctive. All looked like typical college students. They were similar in age, dressed casually, and looked like someone who could have been sitting in the next seat over all semester.

Which, in fact, they had. Unbeknownst to them, the students in Professor Moreland's course had been part of an elaborate experiment.

Throughout the course of the semester, the women pictured in the survey had posed as students in the course. They arrived a few minutes before the lectures began, walked slowly down to the front of the room, and sat where they could be seen by most of their classmates. During the lectures, they sat quietly, listened, and took notes. When the lectures ended, they packed up their things and left the room with everyone else. Other than not being enrolled in the class, there was little that separated them ·from the rest of the students.

There was one more important detail. Each woman attended a different number of class sessions. Professor Moreland's course met forty times over the course of the semester. Woman A showed up to zero classes, Woman B showed up to five, Woman C showed up to ten, and Woman D showed up to fifteen.

It goes without saying that different people find different things attractive. Some people prefer blondes, while others prefer brunettes. Some women like their men tall, dark, and handsome, but others have different preferences (which is good news for the short, pale, and less handsome among us).

So it's not surprising that different students saw the various women differently. Some thought Woman A was a fox, while others preferred Woman C. Some liked Woman B's eyes, while others found Woman D more appealing.

But even with everyone's idiosyncratic opinions, there was a distinct pattern.

Women who had come to class more often were seen as more attractive. The woman who had come to fifteen classes was seen as more attractive than the woman who had come to ten, who was seen as more attractive than the woman who had come to five, and so on.

Seeing someone more frequently made people like them more.

You might wonder whether the woman who came to fifteen classes just happened to be better looking. Maybe she was just naturally more attractive. But this wasn't the case. Students who were not in the class found all of the women equally attractive. Without differential exposure, the four women looked the same.

Could students have gotten to know the frequent attendees better? No again. While the women attended class, they never interacted, verbally or nonverbally, with any of the other students.

Instead, students liked certain women more because they had seen those women more frequently. Students thought the frequent attendees were more attractive and were more interested in getting to know them. All from happening to see those women a few more times in class.

The idea that mere exposure increases liking may seem strange at first, but it has actually been shown in hundreds of experiments. Whether considering faces in a college yearbook, advertising messages, made-up words, fruit juices, and even buildings, the more people see something, the more they like it. Familiarity leads to liking.[5]

And while the notion that seeing something more times makes us like it more is intriguing in itself, there is another aspect of mere exposure that makes it even more interesting. We are completely unaware it occurs.

When students in Moreland's class were asked whether they had seen any of the women before, almost none of them realized they had. And if someone had asked the students whether seeing the women more frequently shaped their opinions, the students would have looked at that person like they were crazy. *Of course not,* the students would have said. *Why would simply seeing someone a couple times more make them seem more attractive?* And yet it did.

Because, whether we realize it or not, we are all students in Moreland's class. We underestimate how much social influence affects our behavior because we don't realize it is happening.

When we look for evidence that social influence shaped our behavior, we often don't see any. We aren't aware of being influenced one way or another, so we assume it didn't happen. But not being aware of influence doesn't mean it didn't occur.

HIDDEN PERSUADERS

Play a quick game with me for a moment. I'm going to give you a memory test. Below is a list of seven words and I want to see how many you can remember. Take as much time as you need to read the list.

Reckless
Furniture
Conceited
Corner
Aloof
Stapler
Stubborn

Before you take the memory test, I'd like you to do something else. Below is a brief description of someone named Donald. Please read the passage and then answer a few quick questions about him.

> *Donald spent a great amount of his time in search of what he liked to call excitement. He has climbed Mount McKinley, shot the Colorado rapids in a kayak, driven in a demolition derby, and piloted a jet-powered boat—without knowing much about boats. He has risked injury, and even death, a number of times. Now he was in search of new excitement. He was thinking, perhaps, he would do some*

skydiving or maybe cross the Atlantic in a sailboat. By the way he acted one could readily guess that Donald was perfectly aware of his ability to do many things well. Other than business engagements, Donald's contacts with people were rather limited. He felt he didn't really need to rely on anyone. Once Donald made up his mind to do something, it was as good as done no matter how long it might take or how difficult it might be. Only rarely did he change his mind, even when it might well have been better if he had.

I realize you've never met Donald before, but based on this description, if you had to pick one word to describe Donald, what would that word be?

When asked a similar question, most people described Donald somewhat negatively. They thought he was reckless and a bit conceited. Crossing the Atlantic in a sailboat is pretty risky, after all, and the fact that he was "aware of his abilities to do many things well" makes him sound a bit full of himself. Others described Donald as stubborn (based on his unwillingness to change his mind) and somewhat aloof (because he didn't rely on anyone). It's not surprising if you described him negatively as well.

But what if I had asked you to remember a different list of words beforehand? Rather than the list above, what if you'd been asked to remember a completely separate set? The description of Donald would be the same, but the memory list would be different. Would your perceptions of Donald have changed?

Of course not, you'd say. *That random list of words has nothing to do with Donald. It's entirely unrelated.* As long as the description of Donald was the same, you would have seen him similarly.

And you'd be wrong.

Because when a different set of people was asked to remember words like "adventurous," "self-confident," "independent," and "persistent" before reading about Donald, it changed how they saw him. Donald now seemed like a much more positive guy. Rather than seeing his crossing the Atlantic as risky, they saw it as adventurous. Rather than seeing his lack of needing others as signaling his aloofness, they saw it as indicating that he was independent.

Same Donald, judged completely differently. Why?

Even though people didn't realize it, thinking about different words while reading about Donald colored the way he seemed. The words activated different ideas in people's minds, which then spilled over to affect their perceptions of him. All without their awareness. And all driven by the power of nonconscious influence.

INVISIBLE INFLUENCE

This book is about the simple, subtle, and often surprising ways that others affect our behavior.

When people think of science, they tend to think about physics or chemistry. Test tubes and microscopes and molecules twisting together to form a double helix. Laboratories with people in white coats and blackboards filled with chicken-scratch equations that look like a Martian took up calligraphy. Ideas you have to be . . . well, a rocket scientist to understand.

But science doesn't just happen in fancy labs. It's happening all around us, each and every day.

We make riskier decisions because someone patted us on the shoulder. We name our child Mia because names like Madison and Sophia were popular recently. Even strangers, or people we may never meet, have a startling impact on our judgments and decisions: our attitudes towards a welfare policy totally shift if we're told it is supported by Democrats versus Republicans (even though the policy is the same in both cases).

Just like atoms bouncing off each other, our social interactions are constantly shaping who we are and what we do. This science, this social science, determines everything from how you got your name to how you ended up picking up this book.

Social influence, though, doesn't just lead us to do the same as others. Like a magnet, others can attract, but they can also repel.

Sometimes we conform, or imitate others around us. But in other cases we diverge, or *avoid* things because other people are doing them. Our older sibling is the smart one, so we become the funny one. We avoid blaring our horn in traffic because we don't want to be one of *those* people.

When do we imitate others and when do we avoid what they are doing? When do peers motivate us to work harder and when do they drive us to give up? And what does all this mean for happiness, health, and success, both at home and at work?

This book will address these and related questions as it delves into the myriad ways others affect everything we do. With the help of some amazing colleagues, I've spent over fifteen years studying the science of social influence. As a professor at the University of Pennsylvania's Wharton School, I've conducted hundreds of experiments, analyzed thousands of competitions, and examined millions of purchases. We've looked at everything from whether your neighbor buying a new car makes you more likely to purchase one to whether losing actually makes NBA teams more likely to win. *Invisible Influence* brings together these, and dozens of other insights, to shed light on the hidden factors that shape behavior.

Chapter 1 explores our human tendency to imitate. Why people follow others, even when they know the answer is wrong. Why one man's soda is another man's pop. How mimicking others can make us better negotiators. And why social influence makes *Harry Potter* and other blockbusters hard to predict, even for industry experts.

Chapter 2 examines the drive for differentiation. Sometimes people jump on the bandwagon and follow others, but just as frequently they jump off once it gets too crowded. We'll discuss why most sports stars have older siblings, why babies all look the same (unless they're ours), and why some people want to stand out, while others are happier blending in.

Chapter 3 starts to explain how these competing tendencies combine. Whether we imitate others or do something different depends in part on *who* those others are. We'll discuss why expensive products have fewer logos, why companies pay celebrities *not* to wear their clothes, and why people pay $300,000 for a watch that doesn't tell time. Why skin tone affects school performance and why small green frogs are the counterfeiters of the animal kingdom.

Chapter 4 examines the tension between familiarity and novelty, and the value of being optimally distinct. We'll learn why prototypical-looking cars sell better, what chickens have in common with the thirtieth president of the United States, and why hurricanes influence the popularity of baby names. Why modern art might seem grating the first time we see it, but why, after looking at a couple Picassos, Kandinskys are more pleasing on the eye.

Chapter 5 illuminates how social influence shapes motivation. Why having other people around makes us faster runners but worse parallel parkers. How our best chance at saving the environment may come from watching our neighbors. What cockroaches can teach us about competition and why losing at halftime makes professional basketball teams more likely to win

Just one note and one request before you dive in.

The science described here can be (and has been) applied to all sorts of practical problems. Helping people get in shape and perform better at work. Saving the environment and getting products and ideas to catch on.

As you read through the chapters, I hope you will be inspired to apply these ideas. Through understanding social influence, we can improve our own lives, and the lives of others. To help, at the end of each chapter we'll discuss common problems people (and companies) often face, and how social influence can help solve them. When it's better to follow the crowd versus go our own way, how we can increase our own influence, and how we can use these ideas to achieve more successful and fulfilling social interactions.

Now the request. Throughout the book we'll discuss how social influence affects people in ways you might never have thought possible. It's tempting to read such research and assume that it doesn't apply to us: *Sure, other people might follow the herd, but not me.*

But while we think social influence doesn't affect us, we're wrong. So please keep an open mind. Through better understanding how influence works, we can harness its power. We all *think* we are alone in a crowd of sheep. But whether we are or not is a different story . . .

1. Monkey See, Monkey Do

What could be easier than matching the length of two lines?

Imagine you were asked to participate in a basic vision test. In front of you is a pair of cards. On the left card is a line. And on the right card are three comparison lines, A, B, and C.

Your job is simple. Just pick the line on the right that is the same length as the target line on the left card. Decide whether line A, line B, or line C is the same length as the target line. Should be easy, right?

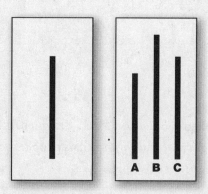

Now let's add one more wrinkle. Rather than doing the experiment alone, you participate with a group of your peers.

You show up at a nondescript building on a university campus, and walk up a flight of stairs to room B7. You see that six other people are already seated around three sides of a square table, so you grab the last remaining chair, the second from the end.

The experimenter gives the instructions. He reiterates that your job is to pick the line on the right that is most similar in length to the one on the left. The group will do a number of trials just like the one above. As the group is small, and the number of trials relatively few, he'll call on each person in turn to announce their choice, which he'll record on a special form.

The experimenter points to the person on the left side of the table and asks him to start. This first participant has red hair, is wearing a grey collared shirt, and seems to be around twenty-five years old. He looks at the same lines you saw on the last page and, without missing a beat, reports his judgment: "Line B," he says. The next participant seems a little older, maybe around twenty-seven, and is dressed more casually. But he reports the same answer. "B," he says. The third person also says B, as does the fourth, and the fifth, and then it gets to you.

"What's your answer?" asks the experimenter. Which line would you pick?

When psychologist Solomon Asch designed this line length study in 1951, he was testing more than people's vision. He was hoping to prove someone wrong.

A few years earlier another psychologist, Muzafer Sherif, had conducted a similar study and found surprising results.[1] Sherif was interested in how norms form—how groups of people come to agree on common ways of seeing the world.

To study this question, he put people in an unusual situation. In a dark room, Sherif displayed a small pinpoint of light on the wall. He asked people to stare at the light and not move their eyes for as long as possible. Then he asked them to report how far the point of light moved.

The point of light was immobile. It didn't move at all.

But for individuals in the room, the light seemed to shift ever so slightly. Gazing at a small dot of light in an otherwise dark room is tougher than it sounds. After staring in the darkness for a while, our eyes fatigue and move involuntarily. This tendency causes the point of light to seem as though it moves even though it doesn't.

Sherif studied this phenomenon, called the autokinetic effect, because he wanted to see how people might rely on others when they were uncertain.

First he put people in the room alone, by themselves. Each person picked a number based on how far they thought the light moved. Some people thought two inches, others thought six inches. Different people's estimates varied widely.

Then, Sherif put those same people into groups.

Rather than making their guesses alone, two or three participants would be in the room at the same time, each making estimates that the others could hear.

People didn't have to agree; they could guess whatever they wanted. But when placed together, what was once a discordant mix of differing views soon became a symphony of similarity. In the presence of their peers, the guesses converged. One participant might have said two inches when she was by herself, while another might have said six inches. But when placed together they soon came to a common estimate. The person who said two inches increased her estimate (to something like three and a half inches) and the person who said six inches decreased his estimate (to something like four inches).

People's estimates conformed to those around them.

This conformity happened even though people were unaware it occurred. When Sherif asked participants whether they were influenced by the judgments of others, most people said no.

And social influence was so strong that it persisted even when people went back to making judgments by themselves. After the group trials, Sherif split people up and had them return to making guesses alone. But people continued to give the answers that they had settled on with the group, even after the group was gone. People who had increased their estimates when others were in the room (from two to four inches, for instance) tended to keep guessing that larger number even when they were by themselves.

The group's influence stuck.

Sherif's findings were controversial. Do people just do whatever others are doing? Are we mindless automatons who simply follow others' every action? Notions of independence and free thought seemed at stake.

But Solomon Asch wasn't convinced.

Asch thought conformity was simply a result of the situation Sherif used. Guessing how far a point of light moved wasn't like asking people whether they like Coke or Pepsi or whether they want butter or cream cheese on their bagel. It was a judgment most people had never made, or even thought of making. Further, the right answer was far from obvious. It wasn't an easy question. It was a hard one.

In sum, the situation was ripe with uncertainty. And when people feel uncertain, relying on others makes sense. Others' opinions provide information. And particularly when people feel unsure, why not take that information into account? When we don't know what to do, listening to others' opinions, and shifting ours based on them, is a reasonable thing to do.

To test whether people conformed because the answer was uncertain, Asch devised a different experiment. Rather than putting people in a situation where the answer was unclear, he wanted to see what they would do when the answer was obvious. When people could easily tell the correct answer right away and thus would have no need to rely on others.

The line-length task was a perfect choice. Even those with poor eyesight could tell the correct answer. They might have to squint a little, but it was right there in front of them. There was no need to rely on anyone else.

Asch thought that when the answer was clear, conformity would be reduced. Drastically. To provide an even stronger test, Asch rigged the group's responses.

There was always one real participant, but Asch filled the rest of the room with actors. Each actor gave predetermined responses. Sometimes they gave the right answer, picking the line on the right that was the same as the one on the left. But on other preselected trials, all of them gave the same wrong answer, saying "Line B," for example, when the answer was clearly line C.

Asch used the line task because he assumed it would reduce

conformity. Real participants could see the right answer, so it shouldn't matter that others gave the wrong response. People should act independently and go with what they saw. Maybe a couple participants would waver once in a while, but for the most part people should give the right answer.

They didn't.

Not even close.

Conformity was rampant. Around 75 percent of participants conformed to the group at least once. And while most people didn't conform on every trial, on average, people conformed a third of the time.

Even though people's own eyes told them the correct answer, they went along with the group. Even when they could clearly tell that the group was incorrect.

Solomon Asch was wrong and Sherif was right. Even when the answer is clear, people still imitate others.[2]

THE POWER OF CONFORMITY

Imagine a hot day. Really hot. So sweltering that the birds won't even sing. You're parched, so you drop into a local fast-food restaurant to grab a cold drink. You walk up to the counter and the clerk asks what you'd like.

What generic term would you use if you wanted a sweetened carbonated beverage? What would you say to the clerk? If you had to fill in the blank "I'd like a _____, please," how would you do it?

People's answers depend a lot on where they grew up. New Yorkers, Philadelphians, or people from the northeastern United States would ask for a "soda." But Minnesotans, Midwesterners, people who grew up in the Great Plains region of the country would probably ask for a "pop." And people from Atlanta, New Orleans, and much of the South would ask for a "Coke." Even if they wanted a Sprite.

(For fun, try ordering a Coke next time you're in the South. The clerk will ask you what kind, and then you can tell them a Sprite, Dr Pepper, root beer, or even a regular Coke.)*

Where we grow up, and the norms and practices of people around us, shape everything from the language we use to the behaviors we engage in. Kids adopt their parents' religious beliefs and college students adopt their roommates' study habits. Whether making simple decisions, like which brand to buy, or more consequential ones, like which career path to pursue, we tend to do as others around us do.

The tendency to imitate is so fundamental that even animals do it.

Vervets are small, cute monkeys found mostly in South Africa. Similar in size to a small dog, they have light-grey bodies, black faces, and a fringe of white around their stomachs. The monkeys live in groups of ten to seventy individuals, with males striking out on their own and changing groups once they reach sexual maturity.

---

* Or imagine you're at the office, chatting with some coworkers. You're about to grab lunch, but the rest of your office mates are on deadline and can't go with you. Being the polite person you are, you ask the group whether you can get them something. How would you address the group— that is, what word(s) would you use to address a group of two or more people? How would you fill in the blank: Would _____ like me to get you anything? The answer seems even easier. But again, it depends on the people around you. People from the West or Northeast tend to say "you guys." People from the South tend to say "y'all." People from Kentucky tend to say "you all." Some people from Philadelphia or Boston might even say "youse," as in "Youse guys want something from the store?"

Scientists often study vervets because of their humanlike characteristics. The monkeys display hypertension, anxiety, and even social and abusive alcohol consumption. Like humans, most prefer drinking in the afternoon, rather than morning, but heavy drinkers will drink even in the morning and some will even drink until they pass out.

In one clever study, researchers conditioned wild vervets to avoid certain foods.[3] Scientists gave the monkeys two trays of corn, one containing pink corn and the other blue corn. For one group of monkeys, the scientists soaked the pink corn in a bitter, repulsive liquid. For another group of monkeys, the researchers flipped the colors—blue tasted bad and pink normal.

Gradually, the monkeys learned to avoid whichever color tasted bad. The first group of monkeys avoided the pink corn while the other group avoided the blue. Just like soda in the Northeast and pop in the Midwest, local norms had been created.

But the scientists weren't just trying to condition the monkeys, they were interested in social influence. What would happen to new, untrained monkeys who joined each group?

To see what would happen, the researchers took the colored corn away and waited a few months until new baby monkeys were born. Then, they placed trays of pink and blue corn in front of the monkeys. Except this time they removed the bad taste. Now the pink corn and the blue corn both tasted fine.

Which would the baby monkeys choose?

Pink and blue corn were just as tasty, so the baby monkeys should have gone after both. But they didn't. Even though the infants weren't around when one color of corn tasted bitter, they imitated the other members of their group. If their mothers avoided the blue corn, they did the same. Some babies even sat on the avoided color to eat the other, ignoring it as potential food.

Conformity was so strong that monkeys who switched groups also switched colors. Some older male monkeys happened to change groups during the study. Some moved from the Pink Avoiders to the Blue Avoiders, and vice versa. And as a result, these monkeys also changed their food preferences. Switchers adopted the local norm, eating whichever color was customary among their new group.

We might have grown up calling carbonated fizzy beverages "soda," but move to a different region of the country and our language starts to shift. A couple years surrounded by people calling it "Coke" and we might find ourselves doing the same. Monkey see, monkey do.

WHY PEOPLE CONFORM

A few years ago, I flew to San Francisco for a consulting project. If you've been to the Bay Area, you know that on any given day the climate can be quite variable. Summers tend not to be that hot and winters don't get terribly cold. But on any particular day, it's hard to know what you're going to get. San Francisco can easily be 70 degrees in November and 50 degrees in July. Indeed, a famous quote about the city—commonly (but erroneously) attributed to Mark Twain—is that "the coldest winter I ever spent was a summer in San Francisco."

My trip happened to take place in November. Since I was traveling from the East Coast, I'd brought my heavy winter coat. But as I got ready to go out that first morning in San Francisco, I faced a dilemma: Should I wear my coat or not? I checked the weather report, which suggested the temperature would be somewhere in the high 50s to low 60s, but I still wasn't sure. That sounded right on the margin between warm and cold. How to decide?

Rather than just guessing myself, I used a time-tested trick: I looked out the window to see what other people were wearing.

When we're not sure about the right thing to do, we look to others to help us figure it out. Imagine looking for a parking spot. After driving around for what seems like forever, you find a whole side of a street free of cars. Success! But excitement quickly turns to concern: *If no one else parked here, maybe I shouldn't, either. There might be street cleaning or some special event that makes parking there illegal.*

If there are even a couple other cars parked on the street, though, the concern disappears. You feel more confident you've found a legitimate spot.

Trying to sort out which dog food to buy or which preschool to send your child to? Knowing what others have done provides insight into what might be best for you. Talking to other dog owners who have similar breeds will help you figure out the right food option for your dog's size and energy level. Talking to other parents will help you figure out which schools have a good student-teacher ratio and provide the right mix of learning and play.

Just as people relied on others to help them figure out how much the light moved in the dark room, we often rely on others to provide a useful source of information that helps us make better decisions.

Using others as information sources saves us time and effort. Rather than giving Fido a new brand of food every week, or spending days reading up on the minutiae of all the preschools in the area, others provide a useful shortcut. A heuristic that simplifies decision making. If other people do it, choose it, or like it, it must be good.

But as the experiment about the length of lines demonstrates, imitation is about more than just information. Even when we know the answer, others' behavior can still have an impact. And the reason is social pressure.

Think about going out to dinner at a nice restaurant with a group of colleagues from work. Business has been great recently, so the boss takes everyone out to celebrate. Some New American place that puts nouveau touches on old favorites. Everything from lobster mac and cheese to un-sloppy Joes made with ahi tuna instead of pork. The appetizers were good, the entrées stellar, and everyone is enjoying a fun evening of drinks and conversation.

Then the time comes to order coffee and dessert. This restaurant is known for their sweets. The key lime pie looks great, but so does the double chocolate cake. Tough choice! You decide to let someone else order first while you mull over the options.

But then something funny happens. No one else wants dessert.

Your first colleague begs off, saying she's too full, and a second colleague says no because he's trying to lose weight. Then, one by one, each person around the table declines.

The waiter gets to you. "Dessert?" he asks.

This situation is a lot like Asch's line-length study. You know what you want—to order dessert, the chocolate cake *and* the key lime pie—just like you knew which line was the correct one. So it's not like other people provide any useful information that helps you make a better decision. But even so, you still feel as though you should pass.

Most people like being liked. We want to be accepted or at least not excluded. If not by everyone, then at least by the people we care about. Anyone who has ever been picked last for a basketball game or left off the invite list to a wedding knows that being left out doesn't feel good.

The same is true for ordering dessert. Sure, you could be the only one to order a tasty treat. There's no law that says you can't eat dessert alone. And yet you feel weird about being the only one ordering. Like people will think you're selfish, or that you'll stand out in a bad way.

So in most cases, people go along. They skip dessert because everyone else passed. Just to be part of the group.

But in addition to information and social pressure there's also one more reason people conform.

CHAMELEONS AND THE SCIENCE OF MIMICRY

Sometimes I look in the mirror and see someone else's face staring back at me.

Most people look like a mix of their parents. Their father's nose and their mom's eyes. Their dad's jawline and their mother's hair.

When I look in the mirror, though—particularly when I've just gotten a haircut—I see my brother. Only five years apart, we look a lot alike. Similar facial structure, similar mouth. My hair is curlier and lighter than his, but we have a lot of the same features.

Genes obviously play a big role. If two people have the same parents, much of their genetic makeup is similar. Depending on which characteristics are expressed, siblings can end up looking like mirror images.

Genetics aren't the only reason siblings look similar, though, because married couples actually resemble one another as well.

Even though spouses aren't related, their faces look alike. Compare two married people with two people selected at random and the married people look more similar.

Part of this similarity is driven by assortative mating. People tend to marry others of similar ages, nationalities, and racial backgrounds. Swedes tend to marry Swedes, twenty-year-olds tend to marry twenty-year olds, and South Africans tend to marry South Africans. Birds of a feather flock together, as they say.

Further, people tend to like others that look like them. If you have an oval face or prominent cheekbones, you tend to find other people with oval faces or prominent cheekbones more attractive. Just like the idea of mere exposure we talked about previously.

All this pushes people toward marrying others that look at least a little like them.

But that's not the end of the story. Because over time, partners' similarity heightens even more. Couples may have started out looking vaguely similar, but as the years go by, the resemblance gets even stronger. It's like two faces morphing into one. By their twenty-fifth wedding anniversary, married people look more and more like proverbial peas in a pod.

And while one could attribute this to age, or shared environment, even controlling for these factors, married people still look more similar than one might expect.

Instead, there is a more subtle mechanism at play.[4] When we feel happy, sad, or any number of other emotions, our faces contort to match our feelings. We smile when we're happy, frown when we're sad, and knit our eyebrows when we're angry.

While any particular emotional expression is fleeting, years of repeated expressions leave their mark on our faces. Crow's-feet, or the tiny wrinkles that form on the outside corners of the eyes, are often called laugh lines because of their association with smiling. It's like folding a piece of paper. The more times you fold it, the deeper the creases become.

But our emotions are not independent. We tend to mimic, or imitate, the emotional expressions of those around us. If your friend laughs while telling a joke, you'll probably laugh as well. And if they share a sad story, your face registers sadness too.

Emotional mimicry is particularly prevalent among married couples. Partners spend a lot of time looking at, and listening to, one another. Hearing what happened at work or empathizing over how frustrating it must have been that the store closed early.

As a result, partners don't just share space and food, they share emotions. They laugh together, cry together, and even get angry together. We might get laugh lines from telling lots of jokes, but our partners are getting those same lines from listening. Years of making the same expressions, at the same time, leave small, but similar, traces on our faces.* Mimicry has made us look similar.

Chameleons are amazing creatures. Unlike most animals, whose eyes move in concert, a chameleon's eyes move independently, allowing them to see almost 360 degrees. Chameleons' tongues are equally impressive. They can be twice a chameleon's body length and when catching prey, lash out at almost 15 miles per hour.

What chameleons are most known for, though, is their ability to change color. To shift their body coloration in response to their environment.[5]

---

* Couples who look more alike over time also report having better marriages. Sharing worries and concerns and repeatedly empathizing with each other boosts satisfaction. But years of subtly mimicking each other has not only made them happier, it's made them look more similar as well.

Humans actually do something similar. We may not change our skin color, but we mimic the facial expressions, gestures, actions, and even language of the people around us.[6]

We smile when others smile, wince when we see others in pain, and say "ya'll" when talking to a friend from Texas. If we happen to be sitting in a meeting where someone touches their face or crosses their legs, we're more likely to touch our face or cross our legs as well. All without realizing that we're doing it.

Mimicry starts almost from the day we're born. Two-day-old babies cry in response to another baby's crying[7] and mimic the emotional expressions of their caregivers. Seeing someone stick out their tongue leads young kids to do the same.

And all this imitation happens nonconsciously. We don't deliberately lean back in our chair if someone else does the same, and we don't try to speak with a Texas drawl just because a friend does.

But even though we may not realize it, we are constantly and automatically imitating the actions of those around us. Subtly moving, posturing, and acting in ways that mirror our interaction partners. And they are doing the same for us.

The neurological underpinnings of mimicry would never have been discovered, though, if it weren't for an ice cream cone.

One hot day in Parma, Italy, a macaque monkey sat in his cage in the corner of a neuroscience laboratory, waiting for researchers to come back from lunch. The monkey was hooked up to a big machine and thin electrodes ran from its brain, registering neural activity. The electrodes focused on the premotor cortex, a region involved in planning and initiating movement. In particular, an area related to actions involving the hands and mouth.

Every time the monkey moved its hands, or mouth, tiny related brain cells would fire, and a sound would register on a monitor.[8] When the monkey raised its hand, the monitor went *bliip, blip*. When the monkey reached out to bring something to its mouth: *bliip, bliip . . . bliip*. The sound echoed through the lab.

So far, the study was going pretty much as expected. Premotor neurons were firing whenever the monkey engaged in various movements. With every action, a loud *bliip* emanated from the machine. The scientists left the equipment on and went to grab a bite to eat.

One of the graduate students returned eating an ice cream cone. He held the cone out in front of him, almost like a microphone.

The monkey looked on with interest. Gazing longingly at the cone.

But then something unusual happened. As the student raised the cone to his lips, the monitor went off. *Bliip, blip,* it sounded.

But the monkey wasn't moving.

The grad student walked closer and again moved the ice cream toward his mouth. *Bliip, bliip,* screamed out the monitor. If the monkey was immobile, why were brain regions associated with planning and initiating movement firing?

Turns out that the same cells that fired when the monkey took an action were also firing when the monkey observed *someone else* take that action.

The cells fired when the monkey moved its hand to its mouth, but also when the monkey merely observed the grad student move the ice cream cone toward his lips. Later tests showed that the cells fired when the monkey picked up a banana, but they also fired when the monkey watched someone else pick up a banana.

The cells even fired for sounds. When the monkey cracked open a peanut but also when it heard someone else crack open a peanut. Observing someone doing something led the monkey's brain to simulate that same action itself. The Italian scientists had discovered what we know today as "mirror neurons."

Since that initial discovery, researchers have found mirror neurons in humans as well. Watching someone else engage in an action activates the same cortical region as engaging in that action. Watch others grab an object, and the motor-evoked potentials, or signal that a muscle is ready to move, is similar to grasping that object ourselves.[9]

Others can thus prime us for action. Observing others do something can activate our mind in ways that make it easier for us to do the same thing. See someone sit up straight in a meeting? Watch someone grab candy from a bowl? We may find ourselves doing the same thing because their actions primed ours. Our minds, and muscles, have been directed down a course of imitation.*

---

* Mirror neurons may have evolved to facilitate knowledge acquisition. Infants are faced with the daunting task of learning hundreds of new things. From smiling and moving limbs to eventually walking and talking. It's as if you've been plopped down at the controls of a spacecraft and suddenly been asked to pilot the thing. Everything is unknown.

Mirror neurons help accelerate learning. Rather than having to figure out how to produce a smile by yourself, watching someone else do it should encourage that action. It should ready the region of the brain that controls an infant's facial muscles to take the necessary steps to produce a smile. And in so doing, make it easier for the infant to do the same.

Learning may also generate mirror neurons in the first place. Before learning, there may be little connection between different sensory neurons coding various actions and the motor neurons responsible for those actions. But through self-observation, or situations in which an adult makes the same expression as an infant, the activation of sensory neurons that observe a behavior and the motor neurons that produce it may become correlated. The simultaneous activation then increases the connection and eventually leads a mirror neuron to form. Neurons that fire together, wire together.

————————

That we're hardwired to imitate is interesting in itself, but behavioral mimicry also has important consequences. Sure, we mimic others, but what happens when others mimic us?

Jake hated negotiating. He hated it so much that he would rather pay full price for a new car than have to haggle. Bargaining for a price on eBay's Make an Offer was enough to give him a small panic attack. Whether sorting out salary requirements at his last job or hashing out the details of a supplier contract, negotiating was something Jake would rather skip. It felt forced, confrontational, and argumentative.

Yet there he was, late one Tuesday afternoon, locked in a tense negotiation over, of all things, a gas station.

Jake had been given the role of service station owner and was facing off against Susan in an MBA class exercise on negotiation. His job was to sell his gas station at a good price.

The owner and his wife had been working eighteen-hour days the past five years to save enough money to realize their life dream: to sail around the world. They'd leave from Los Angeles, and spend two years winding through dozens of places they'd only read about in books. They'd already put a down payment on a beautiful old boat and had started fitting it out for the trip.

The only hitch was the station. They needed money to finance the trip, so would have to sell it. Jake, in his role as the station owner, was trying to unload the station fast. He had to sell it soon, but, to pay for the trip, he had to clear a certain price.

Susan sat across the table.

She had been given the role of representing Texoil, a large oil and gas company interested in buying the station. The company was in the midst of a strategic expansion and was acquiring independent service stations just like Jake's.

Jake started the negotiation by talking about how great the station was. That it had little competition and would be a perfect investment opportunity. Plus, property values had increased over the last decade, and it would cost Texoil much more to build a comparable station from scratch.

Susan flattered Jake by talking about the valued history of the station, but countered that it would require a significant capital investment from Texoil to update. New pumps and a brand-new mechanics area. Texoil could only offer so much for the station.

As negotiators often do, each focused on the facts that made their side look good. They led with why the price should favor their position, and hid information that would hurt their cause.

Eventually, they started tossing out numbers.

Susan offered $410,000. Jake politely declined, and came back with $650,000. Susan budged up a little. Jake countered by lowering his number slightly.

Thirty minutes later, they still hadn't reached a solution.

Negotiation exercises like this one are designed to make students better negotiators. By acting out a real bargaining situation, students get experience feeling out their opponent, deciding how much private information to release, and learning how to close a deal.

But at first glance, this negotiation seemed like a cruel joke. There was no zone of possible agreement.

———

In negotiations, the zone of possible agreement is a range where both the buyer and seller would be happier reaching a deal than walking away. If you're willing to sell your house for anything above $1 million, and a buyer is willing to buy it for anything below $1.2 million, then there is a reasonable range of potential agreement: $200,000. Any offer between $1 million and $1.2 million and the two of you have a deal.

Sure, each of you would like to grab as much of that surplus as possible. As the seller, you'd rather sell it for $1.2 million. You get an extra $200,000 to buy a new car, send your kids to college, or get that Velvet Elvis painting you've always wanted. And the buyer, of course, would rather only pay $1 million. They'd prefer to keep that $200,000 for themselves and put that Velvet Elvis painting up in their own living room. But regardless of how much of the surplus each of you keeps, both of you would rather make a deal within that range than walk away.

In other cases, the zone of possible agreement is much smaller. If you're willing to accept anything over $1 million for your house, and the buyer is only willing to pay up to $1 million, then the bargaining range is pretty tight. The buyer can bluster all they want. They can offer $800,000, $900,000, or even $999,000. But unless they go to the top of their range, the two of you won't reach a deal. No Velvet Elvis for either of you.

As a result, the smaller the bargaining zone, the tougher the negotiation. When there's a large zone, each side can be coy. You can start off at a place that works best for you, but there's still a good shot that a deal can be reached. Tighten that range, though, and reaching an agreement becomes tougher. Each side has to be willing to go further to appease the other. As a result, deals often don't get done.

The Texoil negotiation seemed even worse. It looked like

there was no overlap. The most Texoil had authorized Susan to pay for the station was less than the amount Jake thought he could accept. Either side could go as far to the edge as they were allowed to go and still not reach a deal. It seemed like an exercise in futility.

Fortunately there was a catch.

While the money didn't seem to line up, the underlying interests of the parties were compatible. Sure, Texoil wanted to purchase the station, but they also needed a good manager to run it in the future. And the seller, who had been a great station manager the past five years, wanted to get rid of the station but he also wanted a steady job when he came back from the round-the-world cruise. There was hope.

If both parties could recognize these common interests, and creatively structure a deal, agreement could be reached. They'd have to think beyond just the price of the station itself, though, and incorporate other dimensions. The buyer could offer the high end of their range for the station, but also guarantee the owner a steady job managing the station when he came back from the trip. This arrangement would give the station owner enough money to cover the trip and ensure that he had a job waiting when he returned.

Reaching agreement wasn't impossible. But it required that the parties trust each other enough to reveal otherwise private information. Jake's manager had to reveal that he was selling the station to go on vacation. And Susan's Texoil representative had to reveal that she needed someone to run the station. The seller had to trust the buyer and vice versa.

But trust is the last thing most people feel in a one-off negotiation. Each side is consumed with extracting the most value from the other: how to give up the least information so they can keep the most value for themselves. Saying he was going on vacation might weaken his bargaining position, so people in Jake's position tend not to share.

How could Susan get Jake to trust her? What could she do to win him over and get him to reveal valuable, private information?

Turns out a simple trick led negotiators like Jake and Susan to be five times as successful. Five times as likely to close the deal, even when all seemed lost.[10]

That trick?

Mimicking their negotiation partner.

Researchers wondered whether behavioral mimicry might help the buyer win the seller's trust. They had pairs of Jakes and Susans engage in the same negotiation. But for half the participants, they instructed the buyer to subtly mimic the mannerisms of their negotiation partner. If the seller rubbed their face, the buyer did as well. If the seller leaned back or forward on their chair, the buyer did the same. Not blatantly, but discreetly enough that the other person wouldn't notice.

This might seem silly. After all, why should someone rubbing their face or leaning back in their chair change whether people reach a deal?

But it did. People who mimicked their partner were five times as likely to find a successful outcome. While almost no one who didn't mimic found an acceptable agreement, people who subtly imitated their counterpart reached a deal two-thirds of the time.

Mimicry facilitates social interactions because it generates rapport. Like a social glue, mimicry binds us and bonds us together. Rather than "us versus them," when someone behaves the same way we do, we start to see ourselves as more interconnected. Closer and more interdependent. All without even realizing it.

If someone acts like us, or behaves similarly, we may infer that we have things in common or are part of the same tribe. Part of this may be driven by the association between similarity and kinship. Because we tend to imitate those around us, seeing someone doing the same thing we're doing may serve as a non-conscious signal that we are connected in some way. If someone has the same accent or loves the same brand we feel an affinity or bond. These connections, in turn, lead to greater liking, and smoother interactions.

As a result, mimicry has all sorts of interpersonal consequences.[11] Speed daters whose linguistic styles better mimicked one another were three times more likely to want to see each other again. Existing couples with matching linguistics styles were 50 percent more likely to still be dating three months later.

Mimicry also shapes professional success. In negotiations, mimicry not only helped people reach deals, it enabled negotiators to create value and claim more of that value for themselves. In interviews, mimicry led interviewees to feel more comfortable and perform better. And in a retail context, mimicking increased persuasion.

In fact, the only time we don't mimic others is when we don't want to affiliate with them. People who are satisfied in their current romantic relationship, for example, were less likely to mimic attractive members of the opposite sex. Only when we *don't* want to connect with others do we break from this default tendency.[*]

---

[*] Mimicry is such a standard part of how people interact that lack of imitation makes people feel rejected. When people are told to avoid doing the same thing as their interaction partner, that partner feels a greater need to belong and their hormones spike.

By now it's clear that people often do the same thing as others. But might this penchant for imitation help shape what becomes popular?

WHAT IMITATION CAN TEACH US ABOUT BLOCKBUSTERS

At the beginning, all you see is a foot, slowly tapping against the aluminum leg of a school desk. Then a pencil, drumming on a textbook. And finally, a girl's bored face, head resting on her chin, waiting. Waiting for the clock to strike three p.m.

The seconds slowly drag by: 2:59 and 57 seconds . . . 2:59 and 58 seconds. Each tick blending with the sound of the pencil tapping on the book. The camera pans to students glancing at the clock. When will class be over? Even the teacher can't wait.

Finally, the ringing of the bell breaks the standoff. The students grab their backpacks, jump out of their seats, and flood into the halls.

A quick four-count beat and then it starts. "*Oh baby, baby . . .*" a raspy voice intones. *Bum, bum bum bum bum* follows the beat. "*Oh baby, baby . . .*"

The camera zooms in on a teenager with dirty-blond hair tied in pigtails with pink bows at the end. She's dressed as a Catholic school girl, but more like the Halloween costume than ones in real life. Pressed white dress shirt tied off at her midriff, short black shirt, and tall black stockings. She sashays her hips, and as students pour into the hallways, she and a group of her peers break out into a coordinated dance number.

"*Oh baby, baby, how was I supposed to know . . . ?*

And with that, in early fall 1998, the world met one Britney Jean Spears.

". . . Baby One More Time" was more than just an introduction. It was a breakthrough hit. The song broke international sales records and is one of the best-selling singles of all time. *Billboard* magazine named it the best music video of the 1990s and it was voted the third most influential video in the history of pop music. Britney's album, of the same name, went fourteen times platinum in the United States and sold over 30 million units worldwide. It's the best-selling album by a teenage solo artist, and one of the best-selling albums of all time.

All in all, not a bad start.

But . . . *Baby One More Time* was merely a precursor of things to come. Her second album, *Oops! . . . I Did It Again*, became the fastest-selling female album ever. Her third album debuted as number one on the *Billboard* Top 200.

Whether you like her music or not, Britney Spears is one of the most famous pop icons of the early twenty-first century. In addition to a Grammy, Britney won nine *Billboard* music awards, six MTV Video Music Awards, and was given a star on the Hollywood Walk of Fame. Her tours have grossed over $400 Million, and she is the only artist in history to have both a number one album and a number one single in each of the three decades of her career.

Not too shabby.

But just for a second, let's go back to before all that. Before the tours, before the millions of albums, and before her personal life took a turn for the weird. (Remember Kevin Federline?) Even before . . . *Baby One More Time*.

Imagine for a second that we could rerun the world. That we could go back in time and start things anew.

Would Britney still be popular? Would the Princess of Pop still have hit it big?

It's hard to argue with success. After all, Britney wasn't just some one-hit wonder. With over 100 million albums sold, she is one of the best-selling music artists of all time. There must be something about her that made her so successful, right?

Britney had all the telltale signs of someone who would one day be a star. She started dancing at age three. She won talent shows and appeared in commercials at the same age most of us were still learning basic math. She was even cast in *The All New Mickey Mouse Club*, the showcase of teen stardom that launched the likes of Justin Timberlake and Christina Aguilera. Who could have a pedigree like that and not be successful?

When we look at superstars like Britney Spears, we assume that they are profoundly special. That they have some intrinsic talent or inherent quality that led them to hit it big.

If you ask people in the industry why Britney was so successful, they'll say something similar. That Britney had a unique sound. Sure, maybe she wasn't the best singer ever, but she had something going for her. That, combined with snappy dance moves and the right blend of innocence and sex appeal, made her the perfect pop artist. She became a megastar because of those qualities. If you ran the world again, those same qualities would still make her a hit.

Her success was inevitable.

We make similar assumptions about hit movies, books, and other blockbusters. Why did the *Harry Potter* books sell over 450 million copies? They must be great books. "It has all the makings of a classic," some papers gushed. The "engaging stories" are something "we're wired to respond to," argued others. Books that sell that many copies must just be higher quality than the competition. More interesting. Better written. More appealing.

But could these successes be more random than we think?

If artists such as Britney Spears are just better on some dimension, experts should be able to tell. Sure, Britney's music might not be the best technically, but maybe she has the right pop sound to make a hit. So while the critics might belittle her, hit makers know a knockout when they hear it. Industry executives should be able to tell in advance that she would be a superstar.

Same with *Harry Potter*. It's no Chaucer, but when J. K. Rowling shopped *Harry Potter and the Philosopher's Stone* around to publishers in the mid-1990s, they should have jumped out of their seats to publish it. Just like an oenophile can tell the difference between a decent cabernet and great one, someone who has spent ten years publishing books should be able to separate the wheat from the chaff. Maybe everyday Joes and Janes wouldn't be able to tell, but experts could.

Yet they didn't.

Rowling's original manuscript was rejected by the first twelve publishers who saw it. It was too long, they said. Children's books don't make any money. *Don't quit your day job,* they advised.

And it's not just J. K. Rowling. *Gone with the Wind* was rejected thirty-eight times before it was published. Elvis was told he should go back to driving trucks. Walt Disney was fired early on because he "lacked imagination and had no good ideas."

Harry Potter barely even got published. It wasn't until a publisher happened to give the manuscript to his daughter that something changed. The girl nagged her father over and over for months about how great the book was until he made

Rowling an offer. And made her a multimillionaire in the process.

If hits have an inherent quality that separates them from failures, they should be predictable. Maybe not to you, or to me, but at least to industry experts. To people whose job it is to be able to tell the good stuff from the bad.

But what does it mean that even experts get it wrong?

This question vexed Princeton sociologist Matthew Salganik as he was working on his dissertation. Hit books, songs, and movies are so much more successful than their peers that we tend to see them as qualitatively different.

But if the best are distinctly better than the rest, why do experts have so much trouble identifying them? Why did so many publishers pass up the opportunity to sign J. K. Rowling?

To find out, Salganik and his colleagues set up a simple experiment. They designed a website where people could listen to music and download it for free. No famous songs or well-known bands, just unknown songs from unknown artists. Local acts that were just starting out, or groups that had just put together their first demo. Bands with names like Go Mordecai, Shipwreck Union, and 52 Metro.

The songs were organized in a list, one after the other. People could click on any song, listen to it, and, if they liked it, download it. Song order was shuffled for each listener to ensure that each song received equal attention. More than fourteen thousand people participated.

In addition to the names of the bands and the songs, some people were given information about what previous listeners liked. For each song, they could see how many other people had downloaded it. If 150 people had downloaded "Lockdown" by 52 Metro, for example, the number 150 appeared next to the song.

And just like a best-seller list, for these "social influence" participants the songs were ordered by popularity. The most downloaded song appeared at the top of the list, the next most downloaded second, and so on. The download numbers and song order automatically updated each time a listener downloaded a new song. Then Salganik examined which songs people downloaded.

Simply providing information about others' choices had a big impact. Suddenly people tended to follow their peers. Just like watching a point of light in a dark room, people listened to and downloaded songs that prior listeners had liked.

Popularity became concentrated. The gap between the most and less popular songs increased. Popular songs became more popular and less popular songs got even less attention. The songs stayed the same, but social influence led the best to do better and the worst to do worse.

But Salganik wasn't finished. It was neat to see how people's tendency to imitate others influenced popularity, but that still didn't resolve the prior puzzle. Sure, certain songs or books might be more popular than others, but why couldn't experts armed with market research predict those successes in advance?

To find out, Salganik added one more detail.

It's impossible to rerun the real world. No one can stop time, go back, and see what would happen if things started anew. So instead of rerunning the same world, Salganik created eight different ones. Eight separate worlds, or distinct groups, that looked identical—at least initially.

This decision was key.

The beauty of a good experiment is control. In this case, each of the eight worlds started the same. Everyone had access to the same information. All songs started with zero downloads, and because people were randomly assigned to each world, even the participants in the different words were indistinguishable. So while some people might like punk music, and others might like rap, on average there were an equivalent number of people with each preference in each world. On every dimension possible, then, the worlds started the same.

But while they started the same, each world evolved independently. It was almost as if eight different versions of earth were separately spinning next to one another.

If success were driven by quality alone, each world should end up looking the same. Better songs should be more popular, worse songs should be less popular, and the songs that are popular in one world should be popular in all of them. If 52 Metro's "Lockdown" was the most downloaded song in one world, it should be close to the top of the list in others. On average, preferences across the groups should be the same.

But they weren't.

Song popularity varied widely from one world to the next. 52 Metro's "Lockdown" was the most popular song in one world. In another, one of the least popular. Fortieth out of forty-eight. Almost dead last.

Same song, indistinguishable groups of participants, completely different levels of success. Same initial conditions, different final outcomes.

Why was success so variable?

The reason was social influence. There weren't more punk

lovers in the world where 52 Metro was popular than in the world where it wasn't. But because people tend to follow those who came before them, small, random initial differences snowballed.

To understand why this phenomenon occurs, imagine parking at a county fair. There's no real parking lot per se, or even someone directing traffic, just a big field where people leave their cars. People are generally indifferent about where they park, they just want to go eat cotton candy and ride the Ferris wheel. There are no white lines denoting where individual cars should go, so the first family that drives in can park wherever they want.

The first car that drives up happens to be driven by the West family. They slightly prefer facing west when they park, so they drive in, turn right, and park their car facing west:

Entrance

Then the second family shows up. This family, the Souths, prefer parking facing south rather than west. But their preference is not that strong, and given that the first car is parked facing west, they pull up next to them and face west as well:

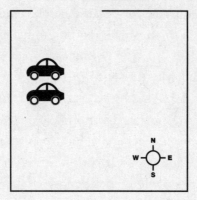

Soon, more and more cars show up. While the people in each might have a slight preference here and there, they follow the cars ahead of them until the parking lot ends up looking like this:

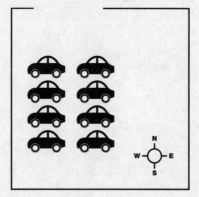

Makes perfect sense.

But what if, rather than the West family showing up first, the South family had shown up first instead? What if the Souths had been the first to park in the lot?

Instead of parking facing west, given the Souths' slight preference for facing south, they go ahead and park that way:

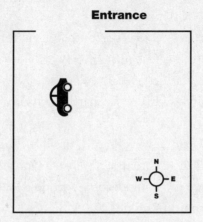

The Wests show up next. They would have slightly preferred to face west, but given a car is already facing south, they go ahead and do the same. More and more cars show up, all following the cars in front of them, until the lot ends up looking like this:

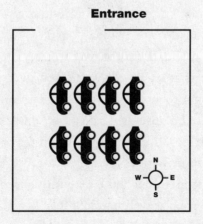

Same eight cars, same overall parking preferences of people in the lot, but completely different outcome. Everyone is facing south rather than west. Just because of the preferences of whoever happened to park first.

This same process drove the outcome of the music study. Imagine two of the social influence worlds at the start of the experiment. They are essentially identical. None of the songs have any downloads. Even the participants are the same, on average.

Just like the Wests and the Souths, though, different individuals may have slightly different preferences. One person may have a slight preference for punk over rap, while another has a slight preference for rap over punk.

And the *order* in which these two people express their preferences varies. In one world, the person who likes punk happens to go first. They listen to a few songs, find a punk song they like, and download it. Score one for the punk song, zero for the rap song. Then, when the second listener comes along, they use the first listeners' choice as a guide. The punk song has more downloads, so it gets more attention. The second listener has a slight preference for rap, but they like punk and the song seems pretty good, so they download it. Punk 2, Rap 0.

In the other world, the person who prefers rap happens to go first. The process is much the same, but with a different outcome. They listen to a few songs, find a rap song they like, and download it. Not because they hate punk songs, but, on the margin, they prefer rap. Punk 0, Rap 1. Then the punk liker comes along, but this time they are second in line. So rather than going with their slight preference, they are influenced by others, and download a rap song as well. Punk 0, Rap 2.

Soon, those two once-identical worlds start to look a little different. One world has a punk rock song on top of the list and the other has a rap song.

Again, one person liking a song isn't enough to entirely change someone else's preferences. But it's enough to tip the scales. Songs at the top of the list got more attention, were more likely to be listened to, and as a result, more likely to be downloaded. Which made it more likely that the punk rock song would be downloaded again in the first world, and that the rap song would be downloaded in the second one. And the process repeated with the next listener.

Slowly, but surely, just like the cars parked in the field, social influence pushed the once-identical worlds in different directions. Magnified over thousands of people making choices, it led to vastly different outcomes.

The implications are both simple and shocking. Rather than being driven by quality, hits might sometimes just be driven by luck and the herd. If we reran the world again, Britney Spears (and J. K. Rowling, for that matter) might never have been popular. Britney's video happened to land at the right time, some people liked it, and, because of that, others jumped on the bandwagon. But she might not be any better than thousands of aspiring musicians we've never heard of.

Does this mean that anything could be a hit? That terrible books and movies are just as likely to be popular as good ones?

Not exactly. Even in Salganik's experiment, quality was still correlated with success. "Better" songs, those downloaded more in the independent world, tended to get more downloads and "worse" songs tended to get fewer. The best songs never did terribly, and the worst songs never did extremely well.

But there was still a lot of variation. And what that means is that quality alone is not always enough.

There are thousands of books, movies, and songs vying for collective attention. And no one has the time to read every book jacket or listen to every sample clip. Most people don't have the bandwidth to check out even a small percentage of the options.

So we use others as a helpful shortcut. A filter. If a book is on the best-seller list, we're more likely to skim the description. If a song is already popular, we're more likely to give it a listen. Following others saves us time and effort and (hopefully) leads us to something we're more likely to enjoy.

Does that mean we'll like *all* those books or songs ourselves? Not necessarily. But we're more likely to check them out and give them a try. And given the thousands of competing options out there, this increased attention is enough to give those items a boost.

Knowing others liked something also encourages people to give it the benefit of the doubt. Appearing on the best-seller list provides an air of credibility.[12] If that many people bought it, it must be good.

J. K. Rowling unintentionally tested these ideas when she released a book under a pseudonym. After her success with *Harry Potter*, Rowling decided to write a detective novel called *The Cuckoo's Calling*. While Potter brought Rowling notoriety, reviewers were critical of later books in the series, and Rowling worried her fame would bias response to the new novel. She wanted to let the writing speak for itself. So she released *The Cuckoo's Calling* as Robert Galbraith. A combination of Robert F. Kennedy and her childhood fantasy name Ella Galbraith.

Robert Galbraith's novel had mixed success. Almost every person who read *The Cuckoo's Calling* liked it. They called it "inspired" and "an engaging read."

Unfortunately, however, there just weren't that many of them. Readers were few and far between. *The Cuckoo's Calling* was released with little fanfare and sold only 1,500 hardcover copies in the first three months of being on sale.

Then one day the book surged from 4,709th to become the best-selling book on Amazon. Soon, hundreds of thousands of copies had been sold.

Had people realized Robert Galbraith's genius? No. Had careful inspection of the writing of *The Cuckoo's Calling* revealed it to be a literary masterpiece? No again.

Someone had simply unmasked Rowling as the book's actual author.

Without J. K. Rowling, *The Cuckoo's Calling* was merely one of the thousands of well-written detective novels competing for attention. With J. K. Rowling, it had a 450-million-copy seal of approval that made potential readers take a look. After all, how could millions of people be wrong?

PUTTING SOCIAL INFLUENCE TO WORK

These findings about the science of imitation have a number of important implications.

When trying to persuade others or convince them to do something, we tend to default to rewards or punishments. The employee of the month gets $100 and their name up on the wall. Kids are told to eat their vegetables or they won't get ice cream for desert.

But while rewards and punishments are effective in the short term, they often undermine what they set out to achieve.

Imagine you were stuck on an alien planet and they serve two things for dinner: Zagwarts and Gallblats. You've never heard of either, and both look a little weird, but you're famished, so you have to eat something.

Before you get a chance to pick one, your host says that before you eat your Zagwarts, you have to eat your Gallblats.

Which one do you think tastes better? Zagwarts or Gallblats?

Kids make similar inferences about ice cream and vegetables. They like ice cream, and while they might not love vegetables, the ice cream reward undermines any otherwise positive feelings they might have had. After all, if vegetables were good in the first place, why would they need a reward to eat them?

An ice cream reward sends a subtle signal that vegetables aren't worth eating on their own. That kids need to be paid (in ice cream) to eat them. And when parents stop paying, kids will stop eating. Whenever they get the opportunity to make their own food choices, vegetables will be tossed to the side. The same goes for employees. They start to infer that the only reason to be on time and give good service is because they'll get paid more, not because they care about their job.

Using social influence is more effective. Just like monkeys with the red and blue corn, people mimic others' choices and actions. If their parents can't seem to get enough broccoli, kids will follow suit.

Unfortunately, many parents signal to their kids that vegetables are not tasty. Parents don't put many vegetables on their own plate, and eat the chicken or steak or whatever else is being served first. And if their parents aren't eating vegetables, why would kids want to?

But if broccoli is the first thing on their parents' plate, and the first thing their parents eat, kids will do the same. Even better if there's a mock argument over which parent gets to eat the last piece. The more kids see their parents eating something—and liking it—the more likely they'll be to do the same.

Mimicry is also a helpful tool.

Imagine you're out to lunch one sunny spring day with a couple of colleagues from work. You're sitting outside at a local pub, and after scanning the menu for a few minutes you know exactly what you're going to get.

The waiter comes by, asks you what you'd like, and the order rolls off your tongue: "The Brussels Burger, medium, with bacon and cheddar, and a side salad."

"Okay," he says, "the Brussels Burger, medium, with bacon and cheddar, and a side salad, correct?"

"Yes," you reply, excitedly. You can already hear your stomach rumbling.

Notice what happened? Probably not.

Yet the same thing happens to each of us dozens, if not hundreds, of times each day. The waiter didn't just take your order, he mimicked you. He could have just said "ok" or "coming right up!" But he didn't. He repeated your order back to you, word-for-word, copying saying the exact thing you said.

Seem trivial? Maybe.

But research shows that this mimicry just increased the waiter's tip by 70 percent.

Whether trying to win a contract, get someone to do something, or just have people like us, subtly mimicking their language and mannerisms is an easy place to start. Even something as simple as mimicking their greeting style (e.g., "Hey," "Hi," or "Hello") in e-mails increases affiliation.

By understanding why people imitate, we can also learn to be less susceptible to influence ourselves.

Group decisions often suffer from something called groupthink, where conformity and the desire for intragroup harmony lead groups to make worse decisions. Watch a focus group share opinions or a committee decide who to hire, and whoever goes first has a big impact on the outcome. Just as how songs became popular due to the preferences of the first few listeners, the direction of the discussion or vote depends on the opinion of whoever happens to lead off. Group members who were on the fence tend to conform, and unless someone has strong objections, they tend to keep their opposition to themselves. Without much of a peep, the group quietly goes one way when they could have just as easily gone the opposite. Groupthink has been blamed for everything from the space shuttle *Challenger* disaster to the Cuban missile crisis.

People talk about the wisdom of crowds, but crowds are only wise when the group has access to everyone's individual information. Aggregating these pieces can lead to better decisions than any person could have made alone. But if everyone just follows everyone else, or keeps their information to themselves, the value of the group is lost.

Consequently, eliciting everyone's idiosyncratic information is vital. So how do we do that? How do we encourage opposing voices to speak up?

Turns out that even one dissenting voice can be enough. If just one prior person in Asch's line experiment gave the correct answer, it was enough to free participants up to give the correct answer themselves. It didn't need to be half the room, just one coconspirator. We don't need to be in the majority to feel comfortable expressing our opinions, we just need to feel like we aren't alone.

Interestingly, the other minority voice doesn't even have to have the *same* opinion. Even a dissenter giving the other incorrect answer (line A rather than line B) was enough to free people up to give the correct answer (line C) themselves. Just having another dissenting voice, even if it didn't agree, made people feel more comfortable in expressing their own personal opinion.

That dissenting voice changed the nature of the discussion. No longer was it right versus wrong, or with the group versus against it. Now the answer was a matter of opinion. And if it's clear that there are different opinions, everyone feels much more comfortable sharing theirs.

To encourage dissenting views, some managers explicitly give one person the job of constantly voicing an opposing perspective. Not only does it encourage people who hold that particular perspective to speak up, it encourages other alternative viewpoints as well.

Privacy also has a powerful effect. "Monkey see, monkey do" nicely describes imitation, but the "Monkey see" part is more important than we often realize. If people can't see, or observe what others are doing, there is no way for those others to influence them. If one monkey never saw whether other monkeys ate the red or blue corn, there'd be no way for the other monkeys' choices to influence theirs. Social influence only works when other people's opinions or behaviors are observable.*

Consequently, one way to break the influence of influence is

---

* This also holds with our own choices. If we want to avoid people influencing our decisions, keeping them private helps. This is why expecting parents often keep their baby's name a secret until the child is born. It avoids the hassle of some uncle linking the name to a little known fungal disease and having to start all over again.

to make choices or opinions private. Using written ballots rather than a show of hands at meetings encourages independence and helps avoid groupthink. Using anonymous ballots makes people feel even freer to speak their mind. Even asking people to write down their preliminary opinion before the meeting can help. It's a small action, but having a written record before interacting with others makes it harder to stray from one's convictions, and increases the chance that diverse viewpoints will be heard.

These same general principles can be used to influence others. One opinion sometimes gets lost in a jumble of voices, but shrink the size of the group and that one voice carries more weight. Rather than trying to sway a whole room, it's much easier to build consensus by going around to each person individually beforehand. By starting with others who agree, it's possible to build a small coalition that can later help win over those who are on the fence.

Going first is also an easy way to shape the discussion. While not everyone may agree, it provides a gravitational attraction, encouraging neutral others to glom on.

These ideas also suggest that the huge lines for Cronuts, Japanese cheesecakes, or whatever else happens to be the food du jour probably aren't worth it. There are almost certainly nearby places that are equally good but don't require a fifty-minute wait.

When searching for cheesesteaks in Philadelphia, tourists are always told to go to Pat's or Geno's. These famous South Philly spots serve thinly sliced rib eye steak on long rolls with provolone, American cheese, or even Cheez Wiz for those so inclined. Late at night or on the weekend, queues out front of these institutions can reach epic proportions.

But are these places really that much better than anything else?

Unlikely. In fact, it's not even clear they are the best.

What they are, though, is prominent. Some number of years ago, through whatever combination of quality and luck, they edged out their peers in being recommended to out-of-towners. And because people who went told their friends, who told their friends, and so on, a small initial difference quickly became magnified, just like in the music experiment.

Nothing draws a crowd like a crowd.

So before spending half the day at Disney World waiting in line for Space Mountain, or camping out overnight to get a new product, we'd be wise to consider the available alternatives. Vacations can sometimes feel like attempting to re-create a highlight reel. Waiting in line at famous site after famous site, fighting the clamoring throng to get that quintessential photo of a bridge or palace. If that's enjoyable, great, but if not, maybe take a peek around the corner. There's probably an equally good place that's not as crowded.

Finally, these findings illustrate the range of things, from trivial to profound, that are shaped by others. We tend to think that we are at the locus of our choices. Our preferences, our predilections, our internal likes and dislikes. But from the food we pick to the language we use to the products that become popular, others have a surprising impact. Ask someone whether their negotiation succeeded because their counterpart mimicked them, and they'd laugh at you like you're crazy. But that influence still shaped success.

It's clear that other people influence our behavior, often without our awareness. But does that influence always lead us to do the same thing? Or might it sometimes lead us to do something different?

2. A Horse of a Different Color

It wasn't there. Sitting in front of the computer at her friend's house, legs dangling off the chair, twelve-year-old Morgan Brian's eyes darted across the computer screen. Frantically she looked up and down the rows of names. First the A team. Then the B team. And finally even the C team.

All of her club teammates were there. Every last one. All ten of them had made one Olympic Development Program team or another. Except for her.

Brian was devastated. She had poured her life into soccer and wanted nothing more than a spot on that team. Even worse, that summer the rest of her teammates went to Montevallo, Alabama, for the regional Olympic Development Program camp, leaving her behind.

It was a tough summer, but it proved a valuable one. Failure became her motivation. Brian worked harder than she ever had before.

She had always been small. So much shorter and skinnier than the older girls she often played with, her teammates nicknamed her "Plankton."

But her size, and skills, soon grew. She played before and after practice, drilling fundamentals with whomever she could find. Chest traps and volleys. Touches with each side of each foot. Repeating the same simple movements again and again until they became second nature.

A year after her failure, Brian made the state team. Then the regional team. And eventually the youth national team. A decade later, she stepped on the field as the youngest member of the U.S. national team. At twenty-two years old, she was one of the linchpins that helped the team win the 2015 Women's World Cup.

A prolific scoring midfielder, Brian has been called the glue that connects the defense to the offense. Some consider her the future of U.S. soccer. America's next big star. A new Mia Hamm in the waiting.

But the first opponent Brian faced wasn't a crafty Brazilian forward or a hardy German defender, it was her older sister, Jennifer. Together they would kick the ball around their parents' front yard until it was time to come in for dinner. Jennifer was five years older, so Morgan didn't win many one-on-one games, but it fueled her interest in the sport.

It turns out that Brian's not the only one. Elite women's soccer players tend not to be firstborn children. Of the twenty-three players on America's 2015 Women's World Cup team, for example, seventeen have older siblings.

Coincidence?

Like any organization, the U.S. national team is interested in predicting which players will do well. What makes some perform better than others? Do certain factors tend to be associated with success?

From the national team itself to the feeder groups that start as young as middle school, slots are limited. There are only so many players that make the cut. But it's tough to pick and choose. How should they pick who to invite and what predicts whether someone will be a national team player someday?

To find out, researchers studied players of all ages.[1] Girls that participated in at least one U.S. women's national team training camp, from the under-fourteen level all the way up to age twenty-three. They measured a variety of factors, from physical capabilities and psychological profile to geography and aspirations.

There were all sorts of intriguing relationships. Successful players tended to live with both parents, their mothers or fathers often volunteered to help the team in some capacity, and their parents often had received post-secondary education.

But beyond all these aspects, one factor stuck out: birth order. Three-fourths of the best players in the country have at least one older brother or sister.

And it's not just soccer. Examination of more than thirty sports across the world found the same pattern. Top athletes tended to be later-born children.[2]

There are many reasons that having an older sibling might make someone better at sports. Watching an older brother or sister provides an early introduction. Older siblings can teach their younger counterparts how to play and serve as inspiration.

Older siblings can also serve as training partners or competitors. It's not called sibling rivalry for nothing. Competing against older, often bigger family members forces younger siblings to develop quickly. They have to cope with being smaller, lighter, and often slower. To keep up with, or even beat, their older siblings, younger siblings have no choice but to learn fast. This natural "playing-up" environment motivates them to take more risks and build their skills.

Interestingly, though, while elite athletes tend to have older siblings, those siblings didn't necessarily play the same sport. These older brothers and sisters were generally active and involved in some sport, just not necessarily the sport at which their younger siblings ended up being successful. Elite soccer players, for example, had older brothers and sisters, but they may have played basketball or volleyball instead of soccer.

So if younger siblings aren't simply learning from, or competing against, their older brother or sister, why are they more successful?

Firstborn children tend to do better academically.[3] They have higher GPAs, score higher on the SAT, and have higher national merit scores. They are more likely to go to college and attend more selective schools.

While some attribute this increased academic achievement to differential parental investment, or the additional resources available to firstborn children, another explanation is more social in nature.

Not surprisingly, firstborn children are almost always the first to attend school. And while not all of them excel in education, many of them at least try to do well. Indeed, firstborns tend to be seen as the studious and conscientious sibling.[4] Not surprisingly then, firstborns tend to be overrepresented in Who's Who lists and among award-winning scientists, including those who have won the Nobel Prize. Firstborns are also overrepresented among world political leaders, including U.S. presidents.[5]

Born into this environment, younger siblings are faced with a choice: They can try to do well in school, like their older brother or sister, or they can seek a different niche. They can follow the trodden path or they can break out and blaze a new one.

And one way to differentiate is to find a different domain to pursue. Consistent with this notion, younger siblings tend to do better in sports. Not only are laterborns overrepresented among elite athletes, they're overrepresented among successful athletes in general.

One study examined the extracurricular activities of over 300,000 incoming college freshmen. Hundreds of thousands of kids at over 550 different schools. Everything from small two-year colleges to large, four-year universities. Though few of these students would ever compete at a national level, the study examined a more middling level of sporting achievement: receiving a varsity letter.

Turns out, good high school athletes tended to have older siblings. Laterborns were more likely to have lettered in high school.[6] Younger siblings were also more likely to spend time discussing sports with their friends.

Whether these lettermen (and -women) had one sibling or three or four didn't seem to matter. What mattered is that they had at least one older brother or sister. Firstborns were less likely to be varsity athletes and only children were even less likely.

Inter sibling differences extend beyond academics and sports.[7] Firstborn children tend to hold more conservative political and social beliefs. They're less likely to support abortion or endorse casual sex. Laterborns, however, tend to be more liberal. They're less likely to attend religious services and more likely to admit to cheating on a test or drinking beer in high school.

It's important not to overgeneralize from these relationships. Many of the differences, while statistically significant, are not huge, and they are averages, not rules. Many younger children are just as smart, or even smarter, than their older siblings. Many older children are good at sports, and even better than their younger siblings. Some firstborns cheat on tests and some younger siblings are more conservative.

But, on average, there are differences. In fact, personality-wise, siblings end up being little more alike than any two people randomly plucked from the population.[8]

Environmental factors have a big impact on personality. By some estimates, half of the variance in personality is described by one's surroundings. Some parenting styles may encourage children to be outgoing, while other styles may encourage kids to be neurotic.

But the data suggest that siblings may actually grow up in quite different environments.[9] The personalities of twins reared together, for example, are not systematically more similar than that of twins reared apart.[10] Adopted siblings grow up in the same household, yet their personalities are almost completely uncor-related.[11]

Parents who feel like their children are as different as night and day might be onto something. One child may be an optimist, while another is a pessimist. One may be the life of the party, while the other is quiet and introverted.

These differences aren't random.

Sibling rivalries are more than just who is better at soccer or who gets the last scoop of ice cream. They're about who gets to be a certain type of person and who has to be someone else. Who is the funny one and who is the brainy one. Who is more like Mom and who is more like Dad.

Siblings encourage both imitation and differentiation. Kids often idolize their older brothers and sisters and end up tagging along to whatever activity they happen to pursue. If an older brother is artsy, their younger sister may follow them to art class or spend more time at the craft shop. All driving the younger sibling to become like the older one.

But while imitation leads younger siblings down the same path as older siblings, they soon learn that this route is taken. It's hard to be the artsy one, funny one, smart one, sporty one, or any of another number of roles if one's older brother or sister already has it locked down. They're the artsy one, so it's not enough just to like art. You have to care that much more, know that much more, or try that much harder to unseat them and claim that domain as your own. Siblings are a salient point of social comparison, and always doing worse doesn't feel so good.

So unless the older sibling moves on to greener pastures, younger siblings often end up going a different way. Whether to stand out to their parents, or themselves, younger siblings try to create their own niche.

This is particularly true among siblings who are similar in age. In three-child families, thirdborns tend to be more similar to firstborns than they are to their next older sibling.[12] Differentiation also ends up being greater among same-sex than opposite sex siblings. Opposite-sex siblings already differ on one major dimension, making it easier for them to be similar on others.

Kids' personalities even seem to shift over time in opposition to their siblings.[13] As one child becomes more extraverted, another becomes more introverted. Like the proverbial yin and yang, as one moves the other moves with it. Forever connected, but forever striving for difference.

Siblings, then, serve an important function. They are playmates and confidants, allies and friends. But they also shape the environment one grows up in. Both as role models and as points of differentiation.

"I think I learned a lot from her," soccer star Morgan Brian said of her sister. "I saw her like soccer but not really pursue it. Maybe I wanted to be the opposite."

THE DRIVE FOR DIFFERENCE

Imagine you're buying a piece of art. You're not usually a big art buyer, but you happened to be walking past a gallery and the piece just drew you in. It's a stunning painting. A bit abstract, but with lush hues, beautiful lines, and gorgeous composition. Part of a limited set of fifteen from the same artist. It just speaks to you and the colors match perfectly with your living room.

A couple of days before you're supposed to finalize the purchase, you happen to drop by your neighbor's house for coffee. The two of you are fairly close friends, so you get together every so often to chat and catch up. He tells you about the vacation he's planning to Florida, you talk about your boss's penchant for falling asleep during important meetings, and the two of you trade opinions about which recent Hollywood blockbuster was best.

Then he brings up art. Heard you were thinking of buying a painting, he says. Before you close the deal on anything, you just have to see what I just bought. It's perfect! We spent forever looking, but in the end we couldn't be happier. I think you'll really like it!

And you do.

You walk outside, he opens the garage, and you behold his gleaming new piece. The very same painting you were going to buy.

Same artist. Same abstract shapes. Same beautiful colors. A couple small differences in layout, but it's basically the same piece.

What would you do? Would you still buy the painting you had in mind or would you look around for something else?

Scientists didn't run this exact experiment (buying paintings would get expensive), but they ran a similar study at a local microbrewery.[14]

Two consumer psychologists posed as waiters doing a beer tasting. They offered groups of patrons sitting together the opportunity to sample one of four house beers: a medium-bodied red ale, a golden lager, an India pale ale, and a Bavarian summer-style beer. Patrons picked whichever one they wanted, and were given a free four-ounce sample to try.

Free beer? Most people were more than happy to participate.

After drinking the beer, customers answered a couple of questions: How much had they liked the beer? Did they wish they had chosen a different one?

There was one additional detail. Half of the tables went through the normal ordering process. The waiter gave them a menu, told them about each beer, and then went around the table, one by one, asking people which beer they wanted.

At the rest of the tables, patrons ordered privately. The waiter still gave them menus, and described each beer, but customers marked down their orders on scraps of paper, folded them, and handed them in so no one else could see what they had ordered.

The two ordering situations were almost identical. Everyone chose from the same set of beers and received the same information. The only difference was whether people knew what others had selected before making their own choice.

But when the researchers analyzed the data, they found a striking gap between the two groups. People who knew what others had ordered were much less satisfied with the beer they chose. And they were three times more likely to regret their choice.

Why? Because many had switched their order to be distinct. They picked a different option than they would normally to avoid ordering the same beer as someone else.

Consider a group of three guys out for a drink. Paul loves pale ale, Larry has his eye on the lager, and Peter wants in on the pale ale as well. If they order privately, no one has any idea what the others ordered, so they just go ahead and choose what they want. Paul and Peter get the pale ale. Larry gets the lager.

But if they go around the table, announcing their order one at a time, those who order later can find themselves in a tough position. Paul orders the pale ale, Larry orders the lager, and then it gets to Peter. He'd like to order the pale ale, but given that Paul already picked it, Peter might feel weird about ordering the same beer. Just as you might not want to buy the same painting as your neighbor.

So Peter might pick a different beer, even though it makes him less happy as a result.*

Sometimes people don't want to be the same as everyone else. Sometimes people want to be different.

I LIKE THEIR OLD STUFF

Today, professional baseball is a full-time job. In addition to playing over 160 games in 7 months, the off-season is filled with prepping for the next season. Some players lift weights to bulk up while others follow a strict diet in an attempt to slim down.

---

* Note that ordering in groups has little impact on whoever orders first. Since no one else went before them, he can still choose whatever he likes and feel distinctive.

Squadrons of coaches, chefs, and exercise gurus design regimens to optimize performance.

But it wasn't always that way. Baseball didn't used to pay as much, so players had to put down the bat and glove during the off-season and find other ways to support their families. Hall of Famer Casey Stengel drove taxicabs. Pitcher Walter Johnson dug postholes for a telephone company. Shortstop Phil Rizzuto worked at a clothing store.

Yogi Berra had a job as a greeter and headwaiter at Ruggeri's, one of the best-known Italian restaurants in St. Louis. Even after he led the Yankees to win the World Series in the 1950s, Berra would don a tuxedo and greet patrons as they entered the restaurant in the off-season.

As salaries increased, players spent more of the off-season on baseball and less on their other pursuits. It wasn't worth risking an injury and jeopardizing their main paycheck.

Ruggeri's also changed. Elevated both by its reputation for good food and Berra's celebrity (even though he no longer worked there), the restaurant became more and more famous.

While the newfound fame was a boon for the restaurant's owners, others were less excited. Berra, for one, stopped going. When asked why by some of his friends, he replied, "Nobody goes there anymore. It's too crowded."[15]

Traditional economics would suggest that what one person chooses shouldn't be influenced by what others are doing. Choosing art or buying a beer should be based on price and quality. So unless the artist tacks on a couple thousand dollars to the painting's price or the brewer starts watering down their beer, people's preferences should remain the same.

If anything, people should *imitate* others. Just like the people trying to guess how far a point of light moved in a dark room, others' choices provide information. The more people who picked something, the better that thing must be. Otherwise, why would so many people pick it? If popularity signals quality, people should pick whatever is popular. We should be more likely to do something when others are already doing it.

But that doesn't always happen. Just like Ruggeri's, people often avoid things when too many other people like them.

"Snob effects" describe cases in which an individual's demand for goods or services is negatively correlated with market demand. The more other people who own or use something, the less interested new people are in buying or using it.

Most of us don't want to be the only one doing something, but if too many people start doing it, we go ahead and do something else. When kale or quinoa becomes too trendy, there's a backlash. And when everyone starts talking about how dots are the new stripes, some of the initial dot wearers move on. Even if it means giving up something they like because others like it as well.

In some instances, the reason is rather practical. Restaurants aren't fun when they're too overcrowded. You have to wait longer to get a table or call further in advance to make a reservation. It's hard to enjoy your meal when you have to yell to be heard above the chatter.

But it's more complicated than that.

Talk to a music lover about a band that just became popular, and they might respond with a familiar refrain: *Asian Spider Monkey? I like their old stuff. Their early albums before they sold out and became so commercial. They had a more authentic sound then. It had more edge to it and was less poppy. It was more real.*

Now, it's possible that Asian Spider Monkey's early music

was truly better. While some artists mature, many run out of good ideas.

But how likely is it that the Beatles, Madonna, and many other successful artists actually sounded better before they became popular? Ever heard someone say they like an *unpopular* band's early stuff?

While it's possible that popularity is creativity-sucking kryptonite, there's a more likely explanation. Regardless of whether its music changes, when a band becomes popular, liking it makes people less unique. If you were one of the twelve bystanders who happened to catch one of Asian Spider Monkey's first coffeehouse shows, you're in a small, select group. No one had heard of them, so—unlike saying you like Dave Matthews Band or Beethoven—saying you liked the Spider Monkey's lilting, offbeat sound was a badge of distinction. People might have thought you were talking about *The Wizard of Oz*, or a weird primate infestation, but liking Asian Spider Monkey made you stand out. It might have been an infestation, but it was *your* infestation, and yours alone.

But if Asian Spider Monkey gets popular, all bets are off.

When they hit the cover of *Rolling Stone*, lots of people start listening. Everyone from indie music heads to fair weather fans. And now a band that was yours and yours alone is everyone's. What once was a sign of uniqueness is now generic and widespread.

What's a true Asian Spider Monkey fan to do?

One option is to drop the band completely. To throw out your concert T-shirt and delete their songs from your playlist.

But that's a bit drastic. After all, you still like their music. And you were there first!

So, rather than dropping the band, many people find a way to maintain their allegiance while finding a new source of distinction: saying they prefer the older stuff.

By saying they like the Spider Monkey's early music, people can maintain their fandom and still be different. And they can one-up all the Johnny-come-lately listeners with an additional source of social currency. Not only do they like the popular band's stuff, just like everyone else, but they are so in the know that they knew about the band before everyone else.

In some instances, a backlash starts even before the thing gets popular. The mere hint that something is gaining steam is enough to make some people dislike it. Might as well get there first before everyone else does.*

WHY DIFFERENCE?

When America sits down to turkey and stuffing every Thanksgiving, most people give little thought to where this holiday came from. If encouraged to think about it, we conjure up what we learned in kindergarten: Pilgrims and Indians, or Plymouth Rock and the *Mayflower*. But beyond the cranberry sauce and prim white bonnets, these early settlers actually had a surprisingly strong impact on American values today.

In September 1620, some one hundred people set sail from England to the New World seeking religious freedom. Many

---

* Some differentiate by taking the contrarian position and hating what everyone else likes. Everyone else might just looooove the compost cookies at Momofuko, but me? I'm not impressed. Most people like Jeff Koons, but I think his stuff is just warmed-over Andy Warhol with a touch of Marcel Duchamp. By actively disliking something everyone else likes, people can differentiate themselves. Using their accumulated knowledge as a way of standing out from the crowd, rather than fitting in.

were part of the English Separatist church, a radical Puritan faction that was unhappy with the limited extent of the Reformation and what they saw as the Roman Catholic practices of the Church of England. After a stint in the Netherlands, these Protestants were looking for a new place to settle. Somewhere with better economic prospects and where they would not lose the English language.

At the time, the clergy mediated almost all relationships between individuals and God. Priests were the only people who had a direct line to the holy. They gave out penance and absolution, interpreted and supplemented scripture, and generally acted as intermediaries. Ritual and ceremony ruled the day.

These early Americans, and the ones that arrived soon after, had a different view. They wanted to empower the common person to take control over his or her destiny, both in the next world, and this one as well.

Rather than simply take the word of priests, they called for men and women to study the Bible and interpret it for themselves. Every person could communicate directly with God through his or her faith, and every person could be his or her own priest. Instead of mindlessly following authority, people were encouraged to think and feel for themselves. To be independent.[16]

This notion of independence, or individualism, proved impactful. It shaped not only the settlers' religious beliefs, but how they interacted with their peers. It influenced not only the founding of the Massachusetts Bay Colony (the Pilgrims who landed at Plymouth Harbor whom we celebrate today) but also the broader roots of American culture that grew from this early seed.

People were free to pursue their own ends, independently of others. To make their own path and go their own way.

Years later, when French historian Alexis de Tocqueville surveyed the New World's burgeoning democratic order, individualism was one of the key themes that emerged. Not a negative selfishness or egotism but "a calm and considered feeling which disposes each citizen to isolate himself from the mass of his fellows."[17] This carried through the Declaration of Independence and the protection of civil liberties outlined in the Constitution and Bill of Rights. People's right to be free of undue influence, and to make their own choices.

To this day, questions of individual independence underlie most of the country's political discourse. How far should the government go to protect people's right to express their individual opinions? At what point does protecting one individual's freedom impinge on another's?

Given the historical premium placed on independence and autonomy, it's not surprising that Americans have come to value differentiation. The freedom to do something different than one's peers. Whether that difference comes in interpreting the word of God or picking a different beer.*

Rather than reflecting external considerations, in America, choice is seen as reflecting one's inner preferences, one's personal wants and desires. But with that freedom comes added responsibility. If choice reflects who someone is, it becomes even more

---

* On the flip side, conformity is often seen negatively. It's viewed as relinquishing personal control or allowing oneself to be pushed around. Novels like George Orwell's *1984* or Ayn Rand's *The Fountainhead* warn of the dangers of assimilation and laud independent thought. Movies present dystopian futures where people are merely interchangeable cogs (until the hero or heroine, distinct from the rest, swoops in to save the day).

important to choose in culturally significant ways. Clothes are not just clothes, they're a statement of who we are. And how better to express independence than to choose something different.

Imagine showing up to a party wearing the same dress as another guest. Or going to work one day and finding yourself wearing the exact same tie as your boss.

Most people would be a good sport about it and laugh, but they'd also probably be embarrassed or find the situation mildly uncomfortable. Because, whether due to one person or one million, feeling overly similar to others often generates a negative emotional reaction. It makes people upset or uneasy.

So we choose things that create a sense of difference. Brands that no one else has heard of or apartments in areas that have yet to become gentrified. Limited-edition T-shirts or vacations to obscure Polynesian islands that are only reachable by outrigger canoe.[18]

Distinction even helps explains the adoption of niche high-tech gadgets. Google Glass was supposed to be the future of wearable computing. An optical head-mounted display that placed a small screen in the user's field of vision, it was labeled one of the best inventions of 2012. It promised to take notes, snap pictures, or get directions, all while being hands-free and liberating people to do what they do best.

This promise, however, ran into obstacles. There were privacy concerns and ethical questions about recording people without their permission. Studies raised issue with the device being distracting and states moved to ban Glass while driving. Some early adopters bragged so much that wearers were termed "glassho%$s" for showing off. Soon, Google Glass began to be seen as a solution in search of a problem (rather than the other way around).

Yet, with all these flaws, people still clamored for the device.

They angled for an invite (it was never publicly available) or bid close to $100,000 just to get their hands on one.

Because buying Glass was more than just about whether it was useful or not. For high-tech innovators, the newest gadget isn't just a productivity tool, it's a tool for differentiation. A way to show they are ahead of everyone else: *Other people might look, act, and sound the same, but not me! I'm a rugged individualist. I'm a special snowflake. I'm different.*

WHO ARE YOU?

There are often rewards for being different. Being more attractive gets you more dates. Being taller gets you picked earlier in pickup basketball.

But uniqueness is about more than just being better than others. Sure, standing out in a positive way feels good. Getting asked out frequently or being picked first makes people feel special. But it's more than that.

Suppose you just got a new job. The first day is orientation and you and the other new hires start by doing a little getting to know each other. An icebreaker to begin the day. The group goes around the room, people introduce themselves, and say a little bit about who they are.

I'm a thirty-six-year-old mother of two.

I'm a Baltimore native who loves the Orioles.

I'm the son of a doctor and an art historian.

How would you introduce yourself? More fundamentally, who are you?

This question is both deeply philosophical and extremely practical, and it's a query we answer either implicitly or explicitly all the time.

From the first day of school to a new job, we're constantly introducing ourselves to others. Providing our name and a little bit of information about how we see our identity.

In today's digital world, introductions are often virtual. One's bio on a website or details on the "About" section of a social media profile. A digital overview that offers a quick sense of who someone is, even without meeting them face-to-face.

Twitter barely provides enough room for a full sentence for people to describe themselves, but users tend to use that limited real estate space in particular ways. Love, for example, is the most frequently used word.[19]

But it's not that people are hopeless romantics. They're using the verb to express their preferences. What they like and what they like doing: *I love dogs. I love watching football. I love my kids.*

Other frequent categories include occupations and roles: *I'm a social media manager. A family man. A professor.*

These introductions are more than just pleasantries. On a deeper level, they're a window into how we see ourselves. How we define who we are among the billions of other people in the world.

While no one likes being categorized, objects and even people gain meaning in relation to other things. If you'd never seen an apple before, someone telling you it was an apple wouldn't be useful. It's only when they describe it in relation to other things you know—*It's a small red or green fruit*—that the nature of an apple becomes clearer. By evoking the category to which an apple belongs (a fruit), meaning is communicated.

Fruit tends to be edible, so an apple must be edible. Fruit tends to be sweet, so an apple is probably sweet. By saying that an apple is a fruit, it implies that it grows out of the ground, can be eaten, and probably has a decent number of vitamins.

But meaning comes not only from what an apple is, but also from what it isn't. Saying an apple is a fruit also implies that an apple is distinct from things that are *not* fruits. It probably doesn't have legs, for instance, and would be bad to use as a piece of furniture. Without some sense of distinction, meaning is unclear.

The same principles apply to how we describe ourselves. If someone says that they are a professor, that provides some sense of who they are. It implies that they have qualities in common with other people who describe themselves as professors. That they probably like reading, enjoy thinking, and may spend a little too much time indoors.

But it also suggests that they are different from those who do not describe themselves as professors. They are probably shorter than people who describe themselves as basketball players and less creative than people that describe themselves as artists.

Because if everyone were a professor, "professor" would be a meaningless category. Simply saying *I'm a human being* doesn't provide much information. It doesn't distinguish someone from the billions of others out there.

Distinction is valuable, then, because it provides definition. If everyone were identical, it would be hard to have any sense of self. Where would that self start and others end? Differentiation helps establish a sense of identity. Delineating both who someone is and isn't.

This often plays out as children become young adults. Up until age twelve or thirteen, children are essentially extensions of their parents. They dress the way their parents dress them, eat what their parents cooked, and live where their parents live. They're not clones of their parents (children certainly talk back or hate particular foods), but they've done little to differentiate themselves.

Part of becoming an adult, though, is about defining a unique self. One that's separate from one's parents. So teens rebel. They become vegan, date bad boys or girls, and generally look bored or revolted whenever their parents pick them up from school.

Teens aren't just trying to piss off their parents (although it might seem that way); they're trying to define themselves as unique and distinct. Creating a boundary where their identity starts and their parents' ends.

THE ILLUSION OF DIFFERENCE

Recently, I was talking to a friend of mine who is a lawyer. He asked what I was working on, and when I told him I was writing a book on social influence, he lamented its impact on his colleagues.

"Everyone wants to be the same," he said. "Young lawyers get a bonus and one of the first things most of them do is buy a BMW."

When I pointed out that he, too, drove a BMW, he took issue with my comment. "Sure," he said, "but they all drive silver BMWs. I drive a *blue* one."

Every choice or decision has different attributes or aspects to it. Cars can be described by their brand, model, color, or a variety of other features. Vacations can be described by what city, state, or country you went to, what hotel you stayed at, and what you did while you were there.

The desire to be different may encourage people to buy more unusual cars (a Volkswagen bus rather than a Toyota Camry) or take more unusual vacations (Anguilla rather than Orlando). But desires for differentiation also encourage people to focus on aspects of their choices that make them *feel* more unique. Even if the actual choices are the same.

Women who wear the same dress to a party may focus on the fact that they are wearing different shoes or are carrying different handbags. BMW drivers may focus on the unique color or feature package that they bought. We attend to, and remember, information that supports our need for differentiation.

Consider the handbags below. Both are from the French luxury brand Longchamp. Both are made mostly out of nylon with leather accents. And, according to their description, both are the perfect size for carrying what you need every day. The only difference between the bags, in fact, is their color.

When I asked people how similar these bags were on a scale of 1 to 100, most thought they were extremely similar. Around a 90.

When I asked them why, they listed many of the same reasons noted above. They're the same size, from the same brand, and so on. People thought they were so similar that some of the respondents thought I must be playing a trick on them.

When I asked people who owned one of these bags the same question, however, I got very different responses.

Not similar at all, the Longchamp owners said. *Look how different the colors are!*

Ask someone to list their most treasured possessions. Their favorite necklace, shirt, or kitchen gadget. Then ask them how many other people own that same item.

Inevitably, people underestimate the number. Sometimes by an order of magnitude. The more something matters to us, the more distinctive we assume it is.

Even better, head over to day care and watch dozens of kids making macaroni art. Or go to the dog park and watch all the puppies chasing each other in circles. As an outsider, they all look very much the same. Sure there are differences here and there, but similarity rules.

Yet, ask a parent about their child, or a pet owner about their dog, and you'll get a different opinion. Their baby is completely different from the rest. Their dog is the most unique animal that has ever walked the face of the Earth. Ever.

In some ways, this is the crux of distinction. Some differences are real. We purchase different brands, espouse different opinions, or go on different vacations from our friends and neighbors. We buy that antique coffee table made out of reclaimed teakwood and railroad ties.

But we also satisfy our thirst for difference using our minds alone. By focusing on ways we're similar to everyone else or ways we're different. That we bought our shirt at the same store where thousands of others bought theirs, or that we bought that particular shade of off-off-grey that few others have.

———

These mental gymnastics help resolve a puzzle that many people feel when they hear about distinction.

Look around the next time you're at the grocery store or waiting for the subway and you'll notice that most people look pretty similar. We all have two eyes, two ears, a nose, and a mouth. We wear similar-looking clothes, eat similar-looking food, and live in similar-looking homes. Yet even in this sea of similarity, we feel unique. Different. Special.

And part of it comes down to the illusion of distinction. We focus on ways we are different, even if at the core we are very much the same.

But does everyone feel the desire for difference to the same degree?

LET'S START A CAR CLUB

Consider the flip of the scenarios earlier in this chapter. Not whether you'd still buy a painting you liked if someone already had it, or still order a beer you wanted if someone already ordered it, but how you'd react if someone copied something *you* were already doing. How you'd react to being imitated.

Imagine you just purchased a new car. You show it to a few friends, and then you find out that one of the friends you showed it to went and bought the same thing. The exact same make and model. How would you feel?

When Northwestern professor Nicole Stephens asked MBA students this question, she got some predictable responses.

Irritated or upset, they replied. They felt betrayed that their friend bought the same car and annoyed that their car was no longer unique. The MBAs felt that someone else doing the same thing as themselves would spoil their differentiation, that it would make their car more generic.

This negative reaction fits with everything we've talked about regarding uniqueness. People like to be somewhat unique, and when that sense of differentiation is threatened, a negative emotional reaction occurs. And, consistent with people's desire to be different, the MBAs were upset when someone else copied them.

Nicole also asked another group of people the same question. This second group was similar to the MBAs in many ways. They were around the same age and, like MBAs, mostly male.

There was only one difference. Rather than being relatively well-off, this second group of people were a bit more blue-collar. Rather than attending a prestigious business school that costs over $100,000 a year, they had working-class jobs.

They were firefighters.

When Nicole asked the firefighters how they would feel if their friend bought the same car, almost none of them said they would be irritated or upset. In fact, when she tabulated the data, she found that their responses were decidedly positive. Rather than being annoyed, they said they would be happy for their friend. It wouldn't bother them at all, they replied, and the friend would get a great car.

As one firefighter put it: "Awesome, let's start a car club!"

Why did firefighters react so differently? Why were they comfortable with being similar while the MBAs were not, and what does that tell us about people's desire to be different?

It wasn't until she got to college that Nicole had realized she had grown up in two worlds. Like her parents and their parents before them, Nicole was born in West Palm Beach, Florida. Her family wasn't rich, but they weren't poor, either. Her father had gone to college to stay out of Vietnam, and later became a fire-fighter and started his own pressure-cleaning business on the side. The business grew and soon he could hire a team of work-ers. Eventually they started washing trucks for post offices all over the area. A whole parking lot would be filled with hundreds of mail trucks, and, as kids, Nicole and her brother would help as a way of making extra spending money.

Her parents taught Nicole to work hard. *Play by the rules, get good grades, and you'll have opportunities.*

So she did. Nicole was a good student, a perfectionist even. She did well in school, won spelling bees, and graduated close to the top of her class.

When it came time to think about college, Nicole knew what she wanted. She had never left Florida, but she dreamed of going to a college like the ones she had seen in the movies. A fancy, small liberal arts school somewhere in New England where people wore sweaters and laughed in the quad as the autumn leaves fell.

Nicole didn't know much about these schools; she just knew she had to go. Florida was fine—nice even—but she didn't want to go to the state school where everyone else was going. She wanted to go somewhere special.

When an acceptance letter came in the mail from Williams College in Williamstown, Massachusetts, Nicole was elated. It was just what she had hoped for.

But her parents weren't convinced. *It's just another school,* they said. *There are fine schools here in Florida where you can get a full schol-arship. Why do you need to go somewhere so expensive? Will it really help you get a better job?* These were sensible questions to ask given the price tag attached.

So Nicole called the alumni office. She was looking for data, statistics, anything that would help her parents see that it would be worth the investment.

The alumni office obliged, and sent her reams and reams of information. Eventually, after listening to Nicole's case, her parents caved. Williams it would be.

As Nicole's freshman year unfolded, Williams was perfect in many ways. Consistently one of the best liberal arts colleges in the country, the college had great classes and amazing professors. Basketball was also one of Nicole's passions, and she played on the varsity team. Life was good.

But at the same time, something seemed off. Something she couldn't put her finger on. She felt well equipped academically, but somehow she didn't feel like she fit in with some of the other students.

In some ways, Nicole knew she was privileged. Growing up, she had played on a basketball team in nearby Riviera Beach, an underresourced area where almost a third of families were below the poverty line. She had been the only white girl on the team, and many of her teammates grew up in unsafe, impoverished neighborhoods. Nicole hadn't wanted for anything and she had a stable and supportive family structure. She was embarrassed that she had so much and her teammates had so little.

Yet, at Williams, Nicole realized that other students had access to opportunities she never knew existed. They had houses in the Hamptons, attended expensive prep schools, and used fancy tutors. Their parents had fancy jobs: they were politicians, doctors, and lawyers. Many had all sorts of family connections going back generations. For Nicole, it was a different level of privilege altogether.

It took Nicole years to put these pieces together and make sense of her experiences, but they helped her see the powerful role that cultural background plays in life. She carried these insights into graduate school, where she began looking more deeply into how gender, race, and social class affect people's experiences and outcomes.

The notion that uniqueness is good is pervasive in American culture. Infants are given their own rooms to foster autonomy. Burger King urges people to "have it your way," and cigarette companies encourage consumers to "choose anything but ordinary." Difference seems to be what is valued.

But does everyone feel that way?

Nicole wasn't so sure. She wondered whether social class might play a role. Whether growing up in a middle-class versus a working-class environment might shape whether people preferred to be similar or different.

To find out, Nicole started by looking at cars. She went to two local shopping centers. One was middle-, if not upper-, class. An outdoor mall filled with expensive stores like Louis Vuitton and Neiman Marcus. A place where, if finding a parking spot was too taxing, you could have your car parked by a valet. A place where patrons looking to refresh their palate could get fresh pressed juice "born out of the idea that in order to find fulfillment and balance each day, modern people need to be armed with a fresh set of tools that are simple, convenient, and tailored to their hectic schedules."

The other shopping center was decidedly working-class. No valet parking, no high-end stores, and no notion that a $9 combination of root juices and celery is what people need to find stability in a crazy world. Just a place where mostly blue-collar people go to get a good deal: the parking lot at Walmart.

Nicole went through each parking lot noting the make and model of each car. For the high-end shopping center: a Nissan Sentra, a BMW 328i, a Volvo S60, and so on. For the Walmart lot, a Toyota Camry, an Acura TL, another Camry, row after row.

Then she counted how many distinct car types there were in each lot. How many different make-and-model combinations there were at both the high-end shopping center and at Walmart.

In places where people want to be unique, there should be more variation. A few people might drive the same make and model, but drivers should spread out and there should be more different types of cars.

In places where people prefer to be more similar, however, there should be more overlap. More people should be more clustered around a smaller set of cars. Rather than thirty distinct makes and models, there might be twenty.

When she tallied the results, Nicole found something similar to what she had found with the firefighters. Compared to the high-end shopping center, there were fewer distinct makes and models in the Walmart lot. More people driving the same cars rather than each person driving something different.* Working-class people preferred more similarity.

---

* One might wonder whether this is less about differentiation preferences and more about what people can afford. Wealthier people can afford a broader range of cars, so maybe there are just fewer makes and models in the Walmart lot because working-class folks can't afford all the high-end cars. While that is certainly part of what is going on, it's not all of it. Car colors reveal a similar pattern. Car brands that cater to the middle class tend to offer their cars in a broader range of colors than brands that tend to cater to the working class. The average BMW, for example, is available in more than twice as many colors as the average Honda. Even dimensions like color show a distinct difference in differentiation.

Turns out that there are differences in the drive for difference. Whether people prefer to be more similar to, or different from, others. People from middle-class backgrounds avoid picking popular items, and when someone else chooses something they already selected, it makes them like that thing less. People from working-class backgrounds, however, don't have as big an aversion to fitting in. They pick more popular items over less popular ones, and someone else choosing something they already selected makes them like it *more*. Less rather than more difference is preferred.*

But it's not only about socioeconomic status. Even among working-class or middle-class individuals, people vary in their needs or preferences for uniqueness.** Some people like popular products and brands while others tend to avoid them. Some try to create a personal image that can't be duplicated, while others are fine being more middle-of-the-road.[20]

---

* Social class has a variety of other interesting effects. Take someone's occupation. One of the first questions people from middle- or upper-class contexts ask when they meet someone is "What do you do?" Among the middle and upper classes, one's job is considered a defining element of who you are. People pick their jobs because it is something they are interested in and passionate about, and they see those choices as expressing them as a person. It's a signal of their identity. But in working-class contexts, "What do you do?" would likely not be one of the first things you'd ask someone. Or if you did, it might offend people. Because, for many working-class individuals, their occupation is a means to an end rather than a signal of identity. It's what they do to pay the bills. It's what they do because they need to provide for their families.

** Working-class individuals are so much more than what they do, and to them, many other dimensions of their life are more important. It would be demeaning to assume that a defining feature of who they are is what they have to do to pay the bills.

Cross-cultural differences also play a role. In America, people say that "the squeaky wheel gets the grease." The person who stands out, or is most noticeable, gets the most attention. In Japan, however, a famous proverb notes that "the nail that stands out gets pounded down." There, fitting in with the group is what is important, and standing out can be a bad thing.

While many Americans see uniqueness as signifying freedom and independence, in East Asian culture, harmony and connectedness are valued more. Being too different from others is seen as deviant and as not being able to get along with the group.

Consistent with these differing norms, research finds that, compared to Americans, Chinese and Korean people choose things that are more similar.[21] Give East Asians the choice between a more common option and a less common one and they'll pick the option that is more common. Ask which images Koreans like best and they'll prefer ones that are less, rather than more, unfamiliar.

Uniqueness, then, is not right or wrong. Good or bad. It's a preference derived from context.

Some contexts encourage differentiation. From an early age, middle- and upper-class American children are taught that they are "special flowers" waiting to bloom. Stars in the making that must express themselves to the world. Not only are these children given many opportunities, but they are given the autonomy, choice, and control to decide which of those possibilities is the right one for them based on their personal preferences. Based on how they see themselves as individuals.[22]

It's natural that children born into these contexts see distinction as the right way to be. That they are different from everyone else and should choose in ways that reflect that.

But not all contexts encourage as much differentiation.

Rather than being different, working-class contexts tend to encourage interdependence. Being a team player rather than being a star. Working-class kids spend more time with family and participate more in hands-on caregiving. Children are taught that "it's not just about you," and that it is essential to be a good part of the whole.[23]

So kids who grow up in working-class families tend to attend to and adjust more to those around them. Standing up for oneself is important, but it's also important to think about the needs of others. Focusing less on the self and more on the collective.

As a result, people from working-class contexts prefer less differentiation. Why would you want to be different from everyone else when everyone else is the family members and friends and others you care about? Wouldn't it be better to share experiences than be alone?

These different preferences also show up in the different worlds people inhabit.[24] Advertisements going after working-class consumers don't urge conformity, but they hint at the importance of attending and relating to others. Think about pitches for a Toyota or Nissan SUV that might appear in *Sports Illustrated*. Research finds that the text is more likely to mention friends and family ("Take family time further") and encourage connecting or combining ("When two great things come together"). The visual imagery is almost ten times as likely to include people.

Ads that target middle-class consumers, however, tend to emphasize distinction. Think about the ads that might appear in *Vogue* or *Bon Appétit*. These ads are more likely to encourage differentiation. They are more likely to describe the product as different ("See the difference") or highlight its uniqueness ("Only one of its kind in the world"). Ads that target middle- to upper-class consumers suggest that by buying this product, you can separate yourself from everyone else.

This variation also appears in retail environments. Take your high-end shopping center or Fifth Avenue–type location. Sure, there are some chains, but there are also lots of one-off individual boutiques, each selling exclusive one-of-a-kind or hand-crafted wares. Stores that cater to people that want things that no one else has.

Even the way the merchandise is presented highlights distinction. A single product set on a pedestal. Set apart and separate from the others. Or a few racks of merchandise, each holding just one size of each piece. As if this were the only medium, patterned, olive-green tank top that ever graced the earth. That after this medium, patterned, olive-green tank top was made, someone said, "This is perfect; there shall never be another one like it."

Working-class shopping areas don't have the same diversity of offerings. More chain stores and institutions that look more similar to one another. Or places that offer slight riffs on familiar favorites.

Same with the merchandise. Stacks of identical green tank tops in various different sizes, next to a similar stack of blue tank tops and a similar stack of yellow tank tops. Rows of identical plates and mugs, with extras packed in above so that everyone who wants one can get it. Similarity, not difference, is what is for sale.

Money explains part of the difference, but it's more complex than that. One could argue that working-class people want that special medium patterned olive-green tank top, they just can't afford it. That they would love to buy a high-end Audi that runs on graphene and is released to only 750 lucky customers a year if only they had the funds.

This explanation is overly simplistic, however, and at its core, assumes that unique is somehow "right." That everyone wants to be unique, but whether they get there or not depends on resources.

Resources certainly afford choices. When you have money, or when you live in a world full of opportunities, you have the option to think about differentiating yourself from others and expressing yourself through your choices. If you don't have resources, or you don't live in a context that affords you choices at every turn, you have a lot less flexibility in expressing yourself that way.

But it's not that people from working-class contexts wish they could be more different from others. Far from it. In that context, more similarity is the norm—and the preference.

There is no right way to be. The context we grow up in shapes both how we behave and how we interpret our behavior. While some people want to see themselves as special snowflakes, some are more than happy to just start a car club.

PUTTING SOCIAL INFLUENCE TO WORK

Differentiation isn't just some quirk felt by teenagers or people wanting to rebel. It's something everyone feels to some degree, albeit in varying shades. After all, it wouldn't really be difference if everyone wanted the same amount of it.

Being aware of how distinction shapes behavior can lead to more satisfying decisions. When ordering food in groups, we'll probably be happier if we stick to our preferred option, even if someone else selects it as well. We won't feel unique, but we can easily order a different drink or focus on how we're different on some other dimension. And rather than being stuck with something we like less, we'll have the rest of the meal to enjoy what we chose.

If we're really worried about it, we can try to be the first one to order. Just signal to the waiter. They'll offer to take our order first and then we won't have to worry about others' choices affecting our own.

We can also design choices, and choice environments, to allow people to distinguish themselves. Apple produces the iPod in a wide range of colors. Some people might prefer blue or red to grey, but once you get into colors like orange and yellow, it's beyond catering to personal preference. (Few people report yellow as their favorite color.) By creating so many variants, though, Apple enables customers to feel distinct even though the product is hugely popular and essentially the same for everyone. Your friend can have a green one, your coworker can have a purple one, your mom can have a blue one, and you can still feel unique because yours is red. It's yours and yours alone.

Distinction also helps explain the success of places like Starbucks. Sure the beans might be a little better or the atmosphere might be a little nicer, but it's still three to four times the price of McDonald's or any of the other places people could easily get coffee. So why are people so happy to pay the higher price?

Starbucks isn't just selling coffee, it's selling a personalized experience. We can get our order customized exactly how we want it. Our Starbucks coffee isn't just the same as the guy or gal who was in front of us in line. It's tailored to our specific unique tastes, with what else than our (mostly) unique name written on the side. It's a four-dollar reminder that we are special and different and not like everyone else. And that's but a small price to pay for feeling distinct.

Social influence, then, seems to push us to be both the same and different. Imitating others and distinguishing ourselves from them. So when is it one versus the other?

Turns out it depends a lot on *who* those others are.

3. Not If *They're* Doing It

"You can't be a nonconformist if you don't drink coffee."

—SOUTH PARK

One morning in early 2010, Nicole Polizzi looked in her mailbox and got a pleasant surprise. Amidst the bills, catalogs, and junk mail, there was a large box. And inside the box was a brand-new Gucci handbag.

The beige and ebony tote was covered with Gucci's famous interlocking G pattern and accented with light-gold hardware. At $900, the bag was one of the hottest that season and would have made any fashionista swoon.

Nicole was even more excited, though, because she hadn't ordered the bag. She had received it for free.

But here's where the story gets interesting. It wasn't a friend of hers that sent the bag, or even Gucci itself. Nicole had been sent the Gucci bag by one of Gucci's competitors.

You might not know Nicole by her real name, but you've probably heard of her nickname, "Snooki." Famous for her crazy rants, trashy clothes, and diminutive stature (4'8"), Snooki rose to prominence as part of MTV's reality show *Jersey Shore*.

The show played to the worst guido and guidette stereotypes.* It starred a group of underemployed twenty-somethings who were often drunk, obnoxious, and prone to bar fights. Muscle-bound guys with orangey fake tans, spikey hair, and a love for fist pumping when their favorite song came on (or for any other good reason). Girls who wore full makeup to the gym, bickered constantly, and thought leopard-skin tights added a touch of class.

Snooki was the best of the worst. She argued that the ocean was salty because it was filled with whale sperm, got into a fist-fight with a high school gym teacher, and put forth amazing opinions on everything from same sex relationships ("Guys are douchebags and I hate them all. They don't know how to treat women, and I feel like this is why the lesbian rate is going up in this country.") to politics ("I don't go tanning anymore because Obama put a 10-percent tax on tanning. I feel like he did that intentionally for us. McCain would never put a 10-percent tax on tanning because he's pale and he would probably want to be tan. Obama doesn't have that problem, obviously.").

Snooki became one of the breakout stars of *Jersey Shore*, and her outlandish personality earned her fame and notoriety. She often appeared on daytime and late-night talk shows, created a spinoff show with her friend "JWoww," and was frequently photographed by tabloids and celebrity magazines.

Given her fame, it's no surprise that fashion houses started

---

* While some people may regard the term "guido" as an ethnic slur, given members of the cast used such terms to refer to themselves, I've retained them here. But sincere apologies to anyone who might find the terms offensive.

sending her free handbags. Product placement is a standard marketing tactic that has been around for more than a hundred years. As a prominent TV star and celebrity, Snooki was seen by hundreds of thousands of eyeballs every week. Companies would send her free handbags to advertise their brands and thus increase their sales. A photo of her in *People* magazine could be seen by millions of people, so getting their handbag in the photo would be a powerful and relatively inexpensive form of advertising.

But free bags from their competitors? Why would fashion houses want to give their competitors more exposure?

It turns out that Snooki wasn't the only *Jersey Shore* cast member having an unusual interaction with a brand. That same year Abercrombie & Fitch offered to pay her costar, Mike "The Situation" Sorrentino, a significant sum of money.

Again, paying famous people to wear clothes from a certain brand is a standard marketing tactic. Actresses receive huge sums to wear dresses from particular designers at the Oscars. Tiffany & Co. paid host Anne Hathaway $750,000 dollars to wear their jewelry at the Academy Awards. The expectation is that such placement will increase sales. Seeing items on their favorite stars will make people want them more.

But Abercrombie & Fitch wasn't offering to pay "The Situation" to wear their clothes. Quite the opposite. They were offering to pay him *not* to wear their clothes.

AN AMATEUR SHERLOCK HOLMES

Suppose you're at a party and looking for someone to talk to. The friend you came with asked you to give them a couple minutes to catch up with a work colleague, so you're on your own, hanging out by the bean dip.

You don't know anyone else there, but two people nearby look like potential conversation partners. One is dressed like an artsy hipster. He's wearing skinny jeans, scuffed leather boots, and a vintage shirt. It seems like he's stepped out of an ad for Urban Outfitters. The other person looks a little more professional. He's wearing a polo shirt, tan khaki pants, and leather boat shoes.

Who would you be more likely to talk to? The hipster or the prep? The American Apparel devotee or the person who looks like they just got off work at Brooks Brothers?

Made your pick? Now take a second to reflect on why you chose the person you did. Why you picked one person over the other.

You probably made inferences about each person based on what he was wearing. The artsy hipster might be from Brooklyn, skew a little liberal, and belong to the creative class. He probably drinks craft beer religiously, loves that new dubstep bluegrass album, and can recommend a good art house film.

You probably made different inferences about the preppy person. They might be from the South (or New England), skew conservative, and be really into college football. He might have gone to private school, worked in finance, or played lacrosse at some point.

Are these wild generalizations? Yes.

Can they dip into overly general stereotypes? Certainly.

Yet we make similar inferences dozens of times a day. Like an amateur Sherlock Holmes, we try to deduce things about the people around us based on their choices. Cars and clothes serve more than just a functional purpose. They act as a silent communication system, signaling information to others.

Think about how hiring works at a large financial services firm. Every time they post a new business analyst position, boatloads of résumés pile in. Hundreds of candidates applying for the same spot. It's hard to know who would be the best fit. Who has the right mix of aptitude and creativity? Which applicant will have the necessary quantitative skills and interact well with clients?

Ideally the company could give each applicant a trial run. Let each candidate perform the job for a couple weeks, measure performance, and pick the top performer. But that's unfeasible.

So companies use signals, like where an applicant went to school, the jobs they held previously, or other readily available information as a proxy for qualities that are difficult to evaluate. A candidate graduated from Brown? That's no guarantee that he or she will do well, but the company makes an educated guess based on what they've observed in the past. If Brown grads tend to perform well, the company will start to use that as a signal of who to hire.

The same holds true for social situations like the party with the bean dip. There's not enough time to ping-pong around, briefly sampling each potential conversation partner before deciding who to talk to. And while we could try collecting information about them from other people we know, that would be laborious and time-consuming.

So instead, we use people's choices as signals of who they are and what they're like. Someone who wears a North Face jacket might be outdoorsy. Someone who uses an Apple laptop might be creative. Research finds that people even make inferences about others based on their shopping lists. Whether someone bought Häagen-Dazs or generic ice cream, for example, influenced others' willingness to let that person babysit their children.[1]

In some ways, these inferences seem silly. Does what ice cream someone bought really provide that much information about whether they'd be a good babysitter? Not really.

But, from another perspective, they make a lot of sense. Without making these, and many similar inferences, life would be a lot more difficult. How else could we get a sense of which person at a party we might enjoy talking to, or which job applicant might be a better fit?

Signals provide an easy shortcut.[2] A way to simplify decision making. We use observable characteristics like how someone dresses, how she talks, or what she drives as a clue to more unobservable characteristics, like whether she'd be fun to grab a beer or go to dinner with. We piece together clues to help us solve the puzzle.

And signals aren't set in stone. They can be revised with new information. If every time we met someone dressed like a hipster he was boring—or, even worse, stole our wallet—we'd probably stop talking to people dressed like that pretty quickly.

But we don't just make inferences about others; we also choose things based on who they are associated with.

Suppose you were asked to vote on a new welfare policy. It offers $800 a month for families with one child and an extra $200 a month for each additional child. In addition, it provides full medical insurance, a job training program, $2,000 in food stamps, extra subsidies for housing and day care, and two years of paid tuition at a community college. Benefits are limited to eight years, but the program would guarantee a job after benefits ended, and would reinstate aid if a family had another child.

Would you be in favor or opposed to such a policy?

When we think about attitudes toward social policies like these, we usually think they are driven by our personal opinions. Our own beliefs about or feelings toward the issues. Some people are more liberal and others are more conservative. So it wouldn't be surprising if conservatives preferred more stringent welfare policies while liberals preferred more generous ones. Indeed, when Stanford professor Geoffrey Cohen examined how people felt about this relatively generous welfare policy, he found that liberals loved it and conservatives hated it.[3]

But Cohen didn't stop there. He also gave some conservatives the same policy, except this time he added just one additional piece of information: that Republicans tended to like it. He told people that the policy was supported by 95 percent of House Republicans and that Republican lawmakers felt that the policy "provides sufficient coverage . . . without undermining a basic work ethic and sense of personal responsibility." Same full medical benefits, same guaranteed job after benefits ended, same generous policy overall.

Conservative should hate this policy. It goes against everything they believe in. In fact, no real-world welfare program at the time was more generous than the policy stated here.

But they didn't. Simply telling conservatives that other Republicans liked the policy was enough to completely switch their views. Now conservatives loved the lavish welfare policy. They didn't just support it, they were extremely in favor of it. All because they thought their party liked it.

If you're liberal, this probably confirms what you've felt for a long time. That Republicans are weak-minded conformists who just do whatever the party says. They don't really think critically about the issues, they just follow the party line. No wonder Republicans have run the country into the ground. Democrats are more thoughtful and pay more attention to the actual issues, right?

But not so fast. Because liberals were just as susceptible to social influence. When just given policy information, liberals preferred the generous welfare policy to a more stringent one. But adding group endorsements completely changed their views. If liberals were told that Republicans liked the generous welfare policy, they said they opposed it. And when liberals were given a stringent welfare policy but told that other Democrats endorsed it, they favored it as well. In fact, they liked it even more than the generous policy in the absence of group information. People's attitudes entirely depended on who the policy was associated with.

When people were asked what drove their policy attitudes, though, their party barely figured in the discussion. They said that the details of the proposal and their own philosophy of government drove their decision. What the typical Democrat or Republican believes? They said it barely mattered at all.

And they were wrong. Because people's attitudes weren't just slightly nudged one way or another depending on group endorsement, their attitudes completely changed based on which party supported or opposed them. Regardless of whether the welfare policy was generous or stringent, conservatives supported the policy if they thought Republicans favored it and opposed it if they thought Democrats favored it. And liberals did the same, albeit following what they thought Democrats supported (and opposing what Republicans liked).

When it came to political views, party was stronger than policy.

WHERE DO SIGNALS COME FROM?

When Honda launched a new compact crossover called the Element, the company tried to appeal to twenty-somethings. The SUV was designed to cater to the adventuresome, with fold-down seats and a back that could fit a kayak or mountain bike. Their ads took a similar approach. They were filled with hip, loud music and cool twenty- and thirty-somethings surfing, snowboarding, and doing other extreme sports.

Clothing company Abercrombie & Fitch also projects a certain image. Their ads show highly sexualized, grey-scale photos of toned adolescents hanging out on the beach or just having fun. Abercrombie stores convey a similar aura. Dim lights, attractive salespeople, and the smell of youthful privilege emanating from the walls.

The message from both companies is clear. Want to be like these people? Buy from us. You're not purchasing a product, you're buying a ticket to a certain lifestyle and everything that comes with it. If you like outdoor sports, the Element is the right car for you. If you want to have a hot bod, or date someone who does, wear Abercrombie.

But do companies have full control over what their brands signal?

Honda pitched the Element as a dorm room on wheels for college-age folks and twenty-somethings looking to haul bikes and surfboards, but it also ended up appealing to other demographics. The Element was just as popular with thirty- and forty-somethings who found it perfect for hauling around children and groceries. And senior citizens loved its easy entry, spacious interior, and relatively low price tag.

Soon the Element stopped signaling hip and started communicating something else.

Something similar happened with Abercrombie. But before returning to their story, we first need to learn about small green frogs.

It's tough being a small male green frog. Life starts as part of a huge floating egg mass with thousands of your brothers and sisters. Hatching happens less than a week later. If you survive being eaten by dragonfly larvae and fish, you soon grow to become a tadpole, competing for algae and whatever else you can get your little amphibian lips on. But as you bulk up, you become more appealing to herons, mallards, and other ducks looking for a snack. Fewer than one of every 250 of your peers survive to become frogs.

Being a full-fledged frog isn't any easier. Now you have to find a mate. And it's a tough market. Ladies aren't looking for love, they're looking for someone with a nice, safe place to lay their eggs. Guys with the best spots might even get to mate multiple times during the season. So, in late spring to early summer, you leave the comforts of your primary wetland habitat and migrate to a breeding site, looking for the best corner of pond you can find.

After much hopping about, you finally see it. There, in the fading light of the afternoon, you find the perfect spot. Shady, nicely vegetated, and not too deep. Time to use your vocal cords and let the ladies know you're single and ready to mingle.

But before you can find Ms. Right Now, you hear a noise.

A throaty *boink* (like the plucking of a loose banjo string) that sounds just like yours, only a bit lower and deeper.

Not good.

Someone has come to steal your territory.

The sounds green frogs make tend to be associated with size. Bigger frogs make deeper noises. And bigger frogs almost always beat smaller frogs in a fight.

So what's a small frog to do? How can you hold on to your spot?

Turns out that small green frogs do something clever. They fib. Just a little bit.

Rather than sending their regular call in response to a large male call, small green frogs switch to something else.[4] Something a little richer and deeper than usual. When faced with a rival that might steal their spot, small green frogs produce a lower-frequency call that makes them sound bigger and tougher than they actually are.

It's like renting a Mercedes for your high school reunion or using a ten-year-old photo as your dating website profile. To help them get what they want, the little frogs bluff.

Now bluffing, in itself, isn't bad. Everyone does it sometimes. Who wouldn't mind being a little hipper, smarter, or wealthier than they actually are? So people buy things that send these desired signals.

But when too many people start bluffing, or enough outsiders do something even for more functional reasons (like senior citizens and the Element), something interesting happens. It starts to change the meaning of that signal.

If lots of non-outdoorsy people start wearing North Face, either because they want to seem adventurous or just because they like the way the clothes fit, the brand may lose its value as a signal of rugged outdoorsmanship. Even worse, people may start to associate the brand with wannabes. Something that signaled one thing may start to signal something else.

And that is what Abercrombie & Fitch was worried about when it saw "The Situation" wearing their clothes on *Jersey Shore*. Their press release stated:

> *We are deeply concerned that Mr. Sorrentino's association with our brand could cause significant damage to our image. We understand that the show is for entertainment purposes, but believe this association is contrary to the aspirational nature of our brand, and may be distressing to many of our fans. We have therefore offered a substantial payment to Michael "The Situation" Sorrentino and the producers of MTV's The Jersey Shore to have the character wear an alternate brand. We have also extended this offer to other members of the cast, and are urgently awaiting a response.*

Companies are usually overjoyed when celebrities wear their clothes. But Abercrombie was worried about what would happen if the *wrong* celebrities started wearing the brand.

Because if lots of *Jersey Shore* wannabes started wearing Abercrombie, then the clothes might stop signaling preppy WASP and start signaling something else. And if that happened, people who wanted to look like preppy WASPs might abandon the brand.

People don't just care about whether others are doing something, or how many others are doing it, they also care about *who* those others are.

GEEKS WEARING WRISTBANDS

The knock on the door was a welcome distraction. Karen had spent the last two hours struggling through her computer science homework and was looking for any excuse for a break. She hoped that Catherine was coming by with a late-night snack, but when she opened the door to her Stanford dorm room, it ended up being two students in yellow shirts.

"We're from the Stanford Cancer Awareness Group," the girl said, before giving Karen a yellow pamphlet. "To educate the community, November is Wear Yellow month at Stanford. We're going door-to-door to remind people of this important disease and to sell these wristbands to raise money." The girl handed Karen a little yellow wristband in a plastic bag. "We're asking for a donation of one dollar or more, in exchange for a wristband, all of which will go to cancer research. If you don't have a dollar, we'll even take a quarter. Every little bit helps. It's a chance to contribute to cancer awareness and show your dorm pride."

"Okay," Karen said, "I'll donate. Just hold the door while I go find a dollar." She went over to her desk, rummaged through the top drawer, and found a crumpled single. "Actually, let me get one for my roommate too," she said. She brought back two dollars and exchanged them for two yellow wristbands.

"Thanks!" the guy said. "We're hoping to sell as many as possible to get the word out about the cause. Please wear the band over the next couple weeks and encourage the other people in your dorm to do the same. It will really help."

"Will do," said Karen, before closing the door and going back to her problem set. "Hope you sell a bunch!"

The following week, Karen was coming back from a sociology review session when she smelled something delicious coming from the lounge. She ducked her head in to see half her dorm mates rifling through different boxes of pizza and the other half frantically circling numbers on sheets of paper.

"What's going on?" she asked one of her neighbors.

"Shh," Lisa said, "they said we're supposed to write our answers down independently. Some sort of survey a couple of business students are doing. Do it and you'll get a free slice of pizza." That sounded like a fair trade, so Karen took a survey from one of the students in charge and started filling it out.

In addition to general questions like how late she went to bed, the survey asked whether she owned and was wearing various cause-related items like a 5k T-shirt or a yellow Livestrong wristband. Karen wasn't wearing a 5k T-shirt, but she was wearing the yellow wristband she had gotten earlier in the week, so she circled "yes" to that one. She filled out a couple more questions, dumped the survey in a pile, and grabbed a slice of pizza.

When asked to describe your average Stanford student, "cool" is not the first word most people would use. "Techie," sure. "Smart," maybe. But "cool" would not be the first adjective. Yet, even among a sea of people studying to be biochemists or playing in the laptop orchestra, there is a hierarchy. And close to the bottom on the coolness totem pole would be SLE.

Structured Liberal Education, or SLE, is Stanford's academic focus dorm. The regular Stanford course load not enough for you? Incoming freshman who love to learn can apply to this special dorm and the extra academics that come with it. SLE students do additional readings, and attend extra lectures on topics such as Indian mythology and Christianity in the Middle Ages. Each fall the dorm performs Greek playwright Aristophanes's *Lysistrata*.

Not surprisingly, students who live in SLE are seen as the geeks on campus. People don't dislike the SLE students, they just don't think they're particularly cool.

How would people react if these "geeks" started doing what they were doing? If the geeks started wearing yellow wristbands, for example, would people like Karen keep wearing one or abandon it to avoid looking like a geek?

To find out, Stanford professor Chip Heath and I got into the wristband business.

First, we went door-to-door in Karen's dorm selling the wristbands.[5] Then, different research assistants returned to the dorm to collect a seemingly unrelated survey that let us measure how many students were wearing the wristbands. (Students will do almost anything for pizza.)

Next, came the geeks. We sold the same wristbands to the geeky academic focus dorm next door, SLE.

Finally, the research assistants returned to Karen's dorm after we sold the wristbands to the geeks to see whether Karen and her dorm mates were still wearing them.

There are many reasons students should have kept wearing the wristbands. The bands were relatively novel and signaled support for a prosocial cause. And it's not like the band was something Karen and company knew nothing about. They were already wearing it. So, learning that the geeks were wearing it provided no new information about whether Karen and her dorm mates would like it themselves. Further, it's one thing to avoid something others are doing, but to give up something you already like? The motivation must be strong.

And it was. Even though the wristband signaled support for a prosocial cause, and even though people already liked and were wearing it, adoption by the geeks led them to abandon the band.

Almost a third of Karen's dorm stopped wearing the wristband once the geeks adopted it.

One might wonder whether students abandoned the band simply because they got bored of them, but that wasn't the case. We also sold wristbands to another dorm on the opposite side of campus. These students owned the wristband for the same length of time, but didn't live anywhere near the geeks, so there was less chance that someone who saw them wearing it would confuse them with one of the geeks. And, sure enough, these students kept wearing the wristbands.

Students didn't get rid of the bands because they were old, or because they didn't work anymore, the students abandoned the wristband because they wanted to avoid looking like a geek.

People diverge to avoid being misidentified or communicating undesired identities. Students ate less candy when they saw an obese person eating a lot, and professionals stopped calling their children Jr. once the practice was adopted by the working class. Minivan sales tanked when they became associated with soccer moms, and tech CEOs wear hoodies rather than suits to avoid looking like, well, a suit.[6]

Misidentification is costly. Wearing a shirt with an indie band like Asian Spider Monkey emblazoned across the front is a great signal. It helps you meet other people that like the same music and maybe even find the perfect mate. ("You like them, too?!")

But if fashionistas start wearing the shirt because they've heard the band is the next big thing, the T-shirt loses its value as a signal. Not only are you no longer unique, but observers don't know whether someone wearing the shirt is an indie rock fan or a fashionista. Whether he loves guitar riffs or Prada's new spring collection. As a result, indie rock fans who wear the shirt may be ignored by potential mates and friends. And they may have to endure people coming up to them wanting to talk about whether black is really the new black.

Misidentification leads us to miss out on desired interactions and endure undesired ones. Even worse, it may lead people to think someone is a poser. A wannabe who copies the style of a subculture but isn't part of it.

Not all misidentification, though, is equal. Think about political affiliations or other groups arrayed on a spectrum. Moving from left to right there are Radicals (far left), Liberals, Moderates, Conservatives, and Reactionaries (far right). Members of each group would prefer to be correctly identified and not confused with other groups. But the penalty of confusion gets larger the further away groups are from one another. Sure, most self-identified liberals would prefer not to be thought of as moderates, but being seen as a conservative would be much worse. And conservatives feel the same way about liberals.

The greater the dissimilarity, then, the greater the cost of misidentification. It's never ideal to be thought of as someone you're not, but the more dissimilar the mistaken identity is, the worse it gets. Most twenty-five-year-olds don't want to seem like they're thirty, but they really don't want to seem like they're thirty-five (or seventeen).

The further the mistaken identity, the higher the cost. Seeming that much younger may lead to missed promotions and not being taken seriously. And seeming that much older may lead to being left off party invitations or emails to join that new kickball league. The further from reality, the more detrimental the mis-identification.

Rather than group identities per se, though, divergence is more about the subtle social characteristics that certain signals convey. Teenagers are unlikely to be confused with forty-year-old business executives, and grizzled members of a motorcycle gang are unlikely to be mistaken for balding accountants. But if accountants start driving Harleys to seem tough, people who see someone driving a Harley will be more likely to infer that the rider shares characteristics with accountants.

Imagine you're eating dinner at Hoffbrau Steakhouse. This family-owned and -operated steakhouse has locations all over Texas, from Amarillo to Dallas. And as one might expect from a Texas steakhouse, Hoffbrau's serves a meat-heavy menu. From the bacon-wrapped filet to the Texas Two Step dinner for two (dual sirloin steaks served on a bed of grilled onions), Hoffbrau's has everything to satisfy even the hungriest cowboy. All grass-fed, hand-cut, seasoned, and grilled to perfection.

You decide on the Smoked Sirloin. Hickory smoked and pepper crusted, it sounds delicious. There's only one choice left: Which size?

You're not feeling all that hungry, and when you look at the menu you see two options: the 12-ounce cut and the 8-ounce Ladies' Cut. Which would you choose? The 12-ounce or the Ladies' Cut ?

For women, this choice is easy. You'd probably pick the Ladies' Cut. Indeed, when researchers gave women a similar choice, around 80 percent of women chose the Ladies' Cut steak.

But what if you're a guy?

You're not that hungry, so you'd probably prefer the smaller steak. Heck, the 12-ounce serving isn't just a couple bites more than the 8-ounce one. It's 50 percent more steak. The choice should be simple, right?

After all, a steak is just a steak. People aren't going to think a guy is a woman just because he orders a Ladies' Cut. So guys should have nothing to worry about.

But when consumer psychologists gave men this choice, 95 percent chose the larger steak.[7] And it's not because they somehow decided they were hungrier than they thought. When researchers relabeled the smaller steak the "Chef's Cut," men were more than happy to chose the smaller size. Men avoided the Ladies' Cut steak because they were worried about being perceived as less masculine.

ACTING WHITE

Growing up in Washington, D.C., in the mid-1980s, Sidney had always done well in school. He wasn't the smartest kid in every class, but he usually did better than most of his peers. His report card was a consistent mix of As and Bs, and his standardized test scores were similarly high. When he took a basic skills test in ninth grade, Sidney scored well above his grade level, reaching college level in science, social studies, and language, and almost college level in reading and math.

By the time he reached eleventh grade, though, Sidney's teachers noticed a disturbing disconnect. Sidney's aptitude was there, but his performance was not. While his standardized test scores remained high, Sidney's grades fizzled, dropping to a C average.

His teachers knew Sidney could do better. He just wasn't

putting in the effort. Why wasn't Sidney living up to his potential?

The racial achievement gap has been well documented. Whether you look at standardized test scores, dropout rates, grade point averages, or college enrollment and completion, African-American (and Hispanic) students often do not score as highly as their white counterparts. On the largest nationally representative assessment of American students, the National Assessment of Educational Progress, African-American students score around 10 percent lower on both reading and math.[8] (Like many of the ideas discussed, these are averages, not absolutes, but, given their persistence, one key to fixing them is understanding why they arise and persist.)

There are numerous reasons for this gap. One is resources. Minority students are more likely to attend underfunded schools. Differential treatment, or discrimination, also plays a role. Whether explicitly or implicitly, some teachers and school administrators set lower standards, are less likely to call on minority students, and more likely to assign them to remedial classes, all of which hurt student achievement.

But, in addition to these traditional explanations, there is an even more complex one.

In the mid-1980s, Professors Signithia Fordham and John Ogbu studied the link between race and academic achievement in a Washington, D.C., high school. The school, given the pseudonym Capitol High, was located in a low-income area of the city, and Sidney was one of the students there. Like every school, Capitol High had a mix of students. Some who did well and some who underperformed.

But when Fordham and Ogbu delved into academic performance, they noticed that identity signaling played a pivotal role. Black students who got good grades or took advanced courses were often ridiculed by their peers for "acting white" or being "Oreos" (black on the outside, white in the middle). Spending time in the library, studying hard, or trying to get good grades was labeled as "white," and thus unacceptable.

The notion that academic excellence was somehow inconsistent with African-American identity was extremely destructive. Like Sidney, many black students had the ability to do well in school, but stopped working hard because they didn't want to be ostracized by their peers.

Students who did perform well worked to camouflage their success. They pretended to be dumb or acted like class clowns so no one could claim that they were trying too hard. One high-achieving student begrudgingly took a test for the school's *It's Academic* team on the condition that even if she scored high enough to make the team, she would not participate. She ended up having one of the highest scores but still stayed away.

As Fordham and Ogbu noted:

> *Black Americans . . . began to define academic success as white people's prerogative, and began to discourage their peers, perhaps unconsciously, from emulating white people in academic striving, i.e. "acting white."*

Not surprisingly, this idea sparked controversy.[9] And Fordham and Ogbu's findings are not without their detractors.

But more recent analyses have provided further support for this idea. Two economists analyzed a nationally representative sample of almost one hundred thousand students and found that the link between school performance and popularity varied by race.[10] For white children, higher grades were associated with higher social status. White students who got all As tended to be more popular than white students who got a mix of As and Bs.

But the relationship between grades and popularity differed for minority students. Blacks and Hispanics who got all As in school tended to be less popular than their peers. Consistent with the notion of acting white, minority students who succeed in school seemed to pay a social penalty for investing in education.

Skin tone also plays a role. If trying hard is seen as "acting white," minority students who look more like whites should be more susceptible to teasing, and try harder to avoid sending undesired signals. Compared to their darker peers, lighter-skinned students might be more concerned about being perceived as "acting white," and, as a result, may not work as hard.

Indeed, light-skinned African-American boys not only feel less socially accepted than their dark-skinned peers, they do worse in school, scoring almost a half a GPA point lower.[11] Latino boys who looked less Latino were more disruptive in class, less likely to complete homework assignments, and had lower grade point averages overall.[12]

And it's not just about race. Despite great advances, women are still underrepresented in the fields of science, technology, engineering, and math (STEM). While women make up almost 60 percent of college graduates, they make up only 24 percent of the workforce in these areas.[13]

But, in addition to resources, discrimination, and other factors, identity signaling also plays a role.[14] Research finds that one reason women are less interested in pursuing fields like math, science, and computer science is because of the identity they associate with those fields. Women think of computer science as dominated by geeky guys who love *Star Trek* and video games. And because that is not an identity to which most women aspire, they may avoid these careers and pursue something else. Identity concerns lead many talented and qualified women who could be great computer scientists or engineers to choose other fields.

Identity signaling even affects whether parents pass on HIV to their children.

In South Africa, billions of dollars have been spent combating HIV and AIDS, yet every year thousands of babies are still born with the virus. Part of the challenge is making sure the right drugs reach remote hospitals across the country, but the most difficult challenge is psychological. Expecting mothers refuse the drugs that might save their babies' lives because they don't want to admit that they are HIV positive. Others infect their children through breast-feeding because they refuse to bottle-feed only, a signal in some regions that you have HIV. Improving public health thus requires more than good medicine. It requires understanding the complex calculus of stigma and meaning.

WHEN PEOPLE DIVERGE

These findings are striking, but one question is why they tend to appear in some areas of life more than others. African-American aren't teased for "acting white" when they use the same pens as Caucasian students and men don't seem to mind using the same brand of paper towels or refrigerators as women. Criminals eat bread, yet that doesn't seem to have stopped the rest of us from eating it. So when is divergence more likely to happen and why?

Just like the nature of divergence itself, the answer lies in the communication of identity. Some choices signal identity more than others.

Take cars. Imagine you're about to meet someone you've never met before and a friend tells you that this person drives a Volvo station wagon. What might you infer about them? Do you have any sense of what they might be like?

What car someone drives doesn't tell you everything about them, but it does suggest certain things (liberalness, for example).

Compare that with paper towels. If someone uses Bounty paper towels, how much does that say about them? Does that provide much insight into whether they are liberal or conservative? Whether they live on the coasts or Middle America? Probably not.

That's because certain choices are seen as more relevant to identity than others.

Part of identity relevance comes down to observability. Unless you snoop around someone's house, it's hard to see what kind of paper towels or dish soap they use. Which makes it hard to use those choices as signals of identity.

What someone wears or drives, though, is much easier to see, and thus much more likely to be used for identity inferences.

Choices are also seen as more identity relevant the less they are based on function. Which paper towels or dish soap someone chooses depends a lot on functional benefits. How well do the paper towels clean? Do they hold up or do they fall apart when you try to use them? For these, and many similar choices, utility is primary. As a result, people don't infer much about identity based on those choices.

But other choices are based less on function and more on taste. Compared to paper towels, hairstyles are not really based on function. Same with cars, for the most part. Sure, a brand-new car is more reliable than a beat-up jalopy. And some cars get better gas mileage than others or seat more people. But most cars will get you from point A to point B just fine. When personal taste dictates choices, we are more likely to infer identity from these choices.

And it's only when choices are seen as signals of identity that people tend to diverge. If people don't infer anything about you based on what paper towels you buy, it doesn't matter who else is buying them. Geeks or hipsters, women or men, you could care less. Criminals might love Bounty and it still wouldn't change your behavior. There's no need to abandon them based on who else they are associated with.

THE $300,000 WATCH THAT DOESN'T TELL TIME

Every spring, movers and shakers in the watch industry converge on Basel, Switzerland, for Baselworld, the industry's annual international expo. Located where the Swiss, French, and German borders meet, Basel is the perfect location for the blend of style and precision that makes up the watch industry. More than one hundred thousand attendees come to view the industry's latest and greatest innovations, from the newest Rolexes to breakthroughs in multifunction operability.

In 2008, Baselworld visitors were treated to a special announcement. Renowned Swiss watchmaker Romain Jerome was releasing something unique. As part of its DNA of Famous Legends collection, Jerome had previously offered a Moon Dust–DNA watch made from fragments of the *Apollo 11* and *Soyuz* space shuttles. Each watch dial featured tiny craters, filled with dust from actual moon rocks and the watch straps were made of fibers from spacesuits worn on the international space station. At more than $15,000, the Moon Dust watches were not cheap.

But Romain Jerome's new watch topped that by a hefty margin. It sported a price tag of $300,000.

Called Day & Night, this new release was extremely high end. Made in part from steel salvaged from the *Titanic*, the watch contained not one, but two separate tourbillions, designed to combat the negative effects of earth's gravity on a watch's accuracy.

There was only one sticking point. Not a sticking point exactly, more like a noteworthy detail.

The watch didn't tell time.

As the company's website boasted, "With no display for the hours, minutes or seconds, the Day & Night offers a new way of measuring time, splitting the universe of time into two fundamentally opposing sections: day versus night." Okay, it told time, but only in terms of whether it was light or dark out.

Useless for most people but perfect for the billionaire who never goes outside and has everything except windows in their house. The watch sold out in less than forty-eight hours.

It's easy to laugh at the folly of the super-rich, but they aren't alone. German watchmaker Erich Lacher takes a similar approach with its Abacus watch. A relative steal at $150, the watch keeps time through a single free-floating ball bearing reminiscent of the maze games you might have played as a kid. When the watch face is parallel to the ground and kept perfectly still, a magnet will pull the bearing to the correct position on the watch, revealing the time. Otherwise it's anyone's guess.

Watches that don't tell time are just one example of afunctional products, or items that directly violate their functional purpose. Single-speed or fixed-gear bicycles are another.

San Francisco is a great biking city. There are lots of hills, but the weather is good and bike lanes are prevalent. There are bikers everywhere. People biking to work, people biking for exercise, and people biking to get wherever they happen to be going.

Take a closer look at some of the bikes, though, and you'll notice something surprising: Many have only one gear. Sure, there are mountain bikes with ten gears and fancier road bikes with twenty-one or even twenty-seven speeds for navigating the toughest hills. But look at what most hipsters are riding and you'll notice they have only one gear. Some are even riding fixies, or fixed-gear bikes where the motion of the pedals is fixed to the motion of the back wheel. When the rear wheel turns, the pedals turn with it, meaning that the rider can't stop pedaling if they want to move forward. And there are no brakes. The only way to brake is by resisting the rotation of the pedals by using your legs to slow the bike's motion down.

Why would someone who lives in the second hilliest city in the world buy a bike with no brakes?

By reducing, or removing, functional benefits, fixed-gear bikes and watches that don't tell time become great signals of identity. Most people buy these products for their functional benefits, so something that explicitly forgoes those benefits sends a clear identity signal. Even a kid can ride a ten-speed bike, but it takes skill to ride a bike with only one gear. Anyone can buy a watch that tells time, but it takes someone with a strong sense of self (and another way to figure out what time it is) to wear a watch that doesn't.

Afunctionality thus induces a cost or barrier to entry. Some costs are monetary. You have to have a lot of money to buy a yacht.

But there are other types of costs as well. Time is a cost. It takes a lot of time and effort to learn about wine or be well versed in French philosophy.

There are opportunity costs. Having cornrows or an eyebrow piercing may make it hard to get a high-paying office job.

And there are costs in terms of pain and dedication. Having washboard abs requires doing hundreds of sit-ups and skipping dessert.

These costs reduce the likelihood of widespread adoption. Most people don't have the money to buy a yacht, the time to study Foucault, or the dedication to renounce carbs.

But these costs also have benefits. They distinguish between insiders and imitators. Between people who know or care about a particular domain and people who don't. You can't just hop on a fixie one day and hope to ride it safely. You have to take the time and effort to learn how to do it right.

Same with pronunciation. Take the name Krzyzewski. Try pronouncing it out loud.

For people who are into college basketball, nothing could be easier. You recognize it as Mike Krzyzewski, coach of the Duke Blue Devils. And you've heard it pronounced hundreds of times by various announcers and friends who either like or hate the team.

But for people who don't follow college basketball, pronouncing the name is like a tongue twister. You have to sound it out letter by letter and end up with something terrible like "Krizz-zee-eew-ski." (The correct pronunciation is something more like "Sh-sheff-ski.") To know how to pronounce Krzyzewski, you have to have watched enough college basketball, or hung out with people who do (or speak fluent Polish). And that time requirement is a cost.

Sure, some people would be happy to spend all day watching college hoops. If you told most sports fans that watching NCAA basketball was "costly," they'd laugh you out of the room. For them it's fun to do.

But not everyone feels the same way. And, regardless of whether you like college hoops or not, the time spent acquiring knowledge in that domain is time that could be spent on something else. So, the time required acts as a cost that separates out those in the know from those who aren't.

Costs also explain why some signals persist. Rather than coming in and out of fashion, why some things stick around.

The more costly something is, the more likely it is to retain its value as a clear and accurate signal. Observers can be pretty sure that someone who owns a yacht is rich and that someone who rides a fixie knows her bikes. Because the more costly something is, the less likely outsiders will be to poach it. And by reducing the likelihood of adoption, costs simultaneously increase a signal's value in distinguishing people who have a certain characteristic from those who don't.

Take Mohawks. Most people would love to seem a little edgy, but they're not willing to shave both sides of their head to do it. It's a jarring look that makes it harder to get a white-collar job and a date. Sure, once celebrities like David Beckham and Cristiano Ronaldo adopted the fauxhawk, a toned-down version of the Mohawk with a smaller spike and no shaved sides, stylish men adopted the cut, but they still weren't willing to go all the way.

And that's why the Mohawk has retained its value as a signal of outsider culture. It's costly enough that mainstream folks won't adopt it. Costly signals are more likely to persist and maintain their meaning.

As Yvan Arpa, the CEO of the company that made the $300,000 watch that doesn't tell time, noted: "Anyone can buy a watch that tells time—only a truly discerning customer can buy one that doesn't."

WHEN CHEAP AND EXPENSIVE LOOK THE SAME

When we asked Matt if he would be willing to fill out a quick survey, he was more than happy to oblige. An undergrad at the University of Texas at Austin, Matt was majoring in communications and hoping to break into the music industry someday. But college was expensive, so he was currently busing tables at a local restaurant to make extra cash. When we offered him $5 in exchange for answering a few questions, he jumped at the chance. He pulled a pen out of his bag, sat down at a nearby table, and started reading the directions:

> We are interested in product perceptions. First, please rate how much you agree or disagree with the following statements about fashion knowledge: I know a lot about fashion, I think about fashion often, etc.

Matt didn't think of himself as into fashion. He didn't know much about clothes, never read up on the latest trends, and could care less about the whole thing. The last "fashionable" shirt he bought was one with a weird shiny pattern that his girlfriend made him buy the last time they went to the mall. He circled the "strongly disagree" option for most of the questions and moved on to the next page.

We are going to show you images of various handbags. For each handbag, please write down how expensive you think it is. Next to each picture, write in a dollar amount based on how much you think it costs.

Handbags? *Wow, definitely don't know much about those,* Matt thought. Nevertheless, he gave it a shot.

The first bag had a logo that said Prada on it, and he remembered hearing something about it being a fancy Italian brand. He wrote down $700. Another was covered in Gucci pattern, so he wrote down $650.

Then he got to a third bag. It was gold in color and looked like it was made of some sort of woven material. But it didn't have any logos on it. It almost looked like one of those cheap bags you buy at beach stores to haul odds and ends when you're on vacation.

Matt wrote $20 next to the picture. After thinking about it for a minute, though, that seemed high. He scratched out $20 and replaced it with $15. Then he moved on to the next bag.

Before the Industrial Revolution, most things were made by hand. Families spun their own cotton and flax and wove them together to make their own textiles. Given the difficulty of forming metal parts, any machines that did exist often used wooden components. Work was manual, hard, and often laborious.

With the development of machine tools, the steam engine, and other technologies a slow, steady shift occurred. The flying shuttle, spinning jenny, and other tools allowed weaving to move out of the home and into larger, more dedicated factories. The cotton gin shrank a year's worth of work into a week. Entrepreneurs began to nurture inventors to create new and more powerful machines.

With these technological changes came a new social class. Not only did standards of living increase, so did social mobility. Until then, status had been relatively static. Wealth was hereditary. Titles passed from generation to generation, and with them, the class it conferred. One was a lord because one's father had been a lord, and his father before him. There were those who owned the land, and those who worked it, and the line between these groups proved difficult to cross.

The Industrial Revolution changed that. Money moved from something you either had or didn't, to something that could be acquired. And you didn't have to own land to do it. With the right combination of wits, courage, and luck, one could amass a small fortune in a short period of time. Wealth became decoupled from social class and the nouveau riche was born.

The nouveau riche, or new rich, described the new social class that emerged from the tumult. Rather than inherited wealth passed down from their upper-class families, these individuals had made their own names. Born into the lower social class, their newfound wealth enabled them to consume goods and services once available only to higher-status individuals.

But simply buying expensive goods wasn't enough. The nouveau riche didn't just want wealth, they wanted the status that comes with it. Wealth is often private. No one but you (and maybe your spouse) knows how much money you have in your bank account. Status, however, is social. It is attained in the eyes of others. The respect of one's peers.

So the nouveau riche engaged in *conspicuous* consumption. Rather than just buying expensive food, high-end dishes, or other private items, they purchased consumer goods that displayed their wealth for everyone to see. Buying goods and services not only for their personal value, but as a way of acquiring status and prestige.

Visible signals facilitate identification. You'd have to be pretty wealthy to buy $10,000 toothpaste, but even if you did, almost no one else would know. Cars and clothes are consumed more publicly, however, making them more common carriers of communication.

Brands further facilitate this process through visible logos and explicit patterns. Wearing fancy sneakers with a large swoosh on the side, or an expensive jacket with Burberry plaid, makes it easier for observers to use these products as signals of identity.

One might expect less overt markers, however, for cheaper goods. Sure, people might want to let others know that they bought something from Burberry, but they might be less keen on broadcasting items bought from Walmart. This idea suggests a positive relationship between price and brand prominence. Cheaper goods should have small (if any) logos and more expensive goods have larger, more prominent ones.

But when professor Morgan Ward and I analyzed hundreds of products, we found a different pattern.[15] We picked two major fashion categories, handbags and sunglasses, and coded hundreds of examples, noting the price and whether the brand name or logo appeared on the product.

For cheap products, the brand was almost never identified. Only two of every ten pairs of sunglasses cheaper than $50, for example, contained a brand name or logo. As price increased, branding became more prominent. Almost nine out of ten pairs of sunglasses between $100 and $300 were branded. But as price increased even further, branding became less prominent. Only three in ten pairs of sunglasses costing more than $500 had a brand name or logo on them.

Rather than a positive relationship between price and branding, it was more like an inverted-U relationship.

Not surprisingly, the lack of logos made the items (and their prices) harder for observers to identify. When we asked people like Matt to guess the prices of different handbags, logos and other explicit branding made all the difference. When products had large logos, observers had some sense of how much the items cost. They didn't get the prices exactly right, but they could differentiate between more expensive items and less expensive ones. They could tell that the Gucci bag was more expensive than the one from the Gap.

But take away the logos and observers had no idea. They couldn't tell the difference between a $2,000 bag and one that cost only $20.*

---

* The same phenomenon occurs in other product categories. T-shirts that said Armani Exchange or Abercrombie & Fitch on the front were easy for people to identify. Even shirts with more moderate branding (for example,

If people care about conspicuous consumption, why would anyone pay thousands of dollars for something most observers would think is cheap?

One could argue that people buy expensive brands because they are higher quality, but that can't explain the price premium luxury brands charge for less prominent branding. More expensive Mercedes cars, for example, have a smaller emblem on the hood. For every $5,000 increase in price, the logo shrinks by a centimeter. Gucci handbags and Louis Vuitton shoes show the same pattern. Luxury items with less prominent logos are more expensive. Quieter signals cost more.

Do rich people just dislike logos?

While some products scream the brand for everyone to see, other products have signals that are less blatant. Christian Louboutin uses red soles on all of its shoes, and Coton Doux shirts often have a distinctive pattern around the collar or under the cuffs. One leather brand uses a particular cross-hatched leather pattern on many of its handbags, tote bags, and wallets.

More obvious brand names and logos more effectively communicate to a broad audience (because they are easier to see and identify), but subtle signals may be missed. Most people don't notice the soles of others' shoes, and understated detailing may go undetected. Such "dog whistle" fashion may fail to be decoded by most observers.

---

a small "A|X" logo) were correctly identified around 75 percent of the time. But shirts without prominent branding were much harder to identify. Only 6 percent of observers correctly guessed the brand.

But while this inability to signal widely may seem like a downside, it also has a hidden benefit. Loud signals are easier to identify, but as a result, they're also more likely to be poached or copied by outsiders.

Carrying a handbag that says Louis Vuitton all over it encourages observers to think you're wealthy. But because they're more recognizable, such explicit signals are also more likely to be imitated by people who aren't wealthy, but just want to *seem* that way.

Consider the types of products that tend to be counterfeited. Walk down Canal Street in New York City, or browse websites that specialize in counterfeit items, and not all handbags are represented. Louder bags are more likely to be copied. Bags with larger logos or more explicit branding are more likely to be pirated, because what counterfeit buyers want is the signal. They care less about quality, and more about what the bag communicates.

Consequently, insiders, or people who know a lot about a given domain, prefer subtle signals. They aren't as widely observable, but they help distinguish insiders from wannabes. If people who want to seem rich buy handbags bathed in Louis Vuitton logos, those are no longer a good signal of wealth. So the truly wealthy may diverge and use more discreet markers that only other insiders can recognize.

Even though most people can't recognize them, subtle signals provide a covert communication system with others in the know. Many people would miss Bottega Veneta's pattern, but fashionistas possess the expertise to recognize the understated markings.[16]

Indeed, when we asked fashion students to estimate the price of the bags, they didn't have the same difficulty Matt did. Not only could they accurately estimate the price of the logoed bags, but they could distinguish among the subtly marked bags. Even without large logos, they could separate the expensive bags from the cheap ones.

Rolexes are a widely recognized status symbol. But because of that, true watch aficionados usually prefer something a bit more under the radar. A Vacheron Constantin will be invisible to most people, but other watch lovers will detect the signal and admire the choice.

Remember that plain-looking bag Matt thought was $15? It's actually a $6,000 Bottega Veneta. But while most regular students missed the subtle signals, true fashionistas recognized the brand right away.

And this brings us to the benefits of counterfeiting.

WHY LOUIS VUITTON SHOULD ENCOURAGE COUNTERFEITING

If you've never seen a Louis Vuitton trash bag, you're in for a treat.

No, not Louis Vuitton's Raindrop Besace, a $1,960 waterproof purse that looks like it's made of trash bag material. A real trash bag. One designed for taking out the trash.

These brown bags, adorned with LV's famous gold quatrefoil-and-flowers pattern, are the perfect gift for any friend who prefers the finer things in life. For the person who thinks his or her trash is better than everyone else's.

But before you wonder what the world is coming to, take a closer look. Notice that the bag is missing the distinctive "LV" initials that make up the standard monogram design. Look closer and you'll see that the initials on the bag actually read "VO."

These bags aren't made by Louis Vuitton at all. They're fake.

From Louis Vuitton to Lego, and Rolex to Ray-Ban, nearly 10 percent of worldwide trade is in fake goods.[17] Half a trillion dollars a year that should be going to major companies and brands is instead going to criminals. That's more than the annual production of Norway, Poland, or Belgium. In America alone, counterfeiting costs businesses more than $200 billion a year. In the late 1990s, lighter company Zippo lost one-third of its revenue to counterfeiters.

But it's not just lost revenue. As consumers experience quality issues with fake goods, brand reputations suffer. As counterfeit items proliferate, exclusivity erodes. And the availability of cheap alternatives hurts consumers' willingness to pay full price for a brand's legitimate offerings.

Visit any major port around the world and you'll see the extent of the problem. Shipping containers labeled HOME AND GARDEN are filled with thousands of fake handbags. Material that should be for building supplies ends up being boxes upon boxes of counterfeit sneakers.

The Internet has only facilitated distribution. Now counterfeiters sell direct to consumers. Customs officials try to shut down websites that facilitate these transactions, but new ones pop up quickly. And it's not just small fly-by-night operations, either. A 2008 study found that almost all Louis Vuitton bags and Dior perfumes sold on eBay were fake.[18] Eight in ten products that look like they are from Tiffany & Co. were actually counterfeit. It's an ocean of illegal goods.

Not surprisingly, fashion companies have worked hard to deter counterfeiters. Some brands, like Louis Vuitton, try to trademark designs like their repeating "LV" pattern. Other companies develop products that are harder to imitate. Dolce & Gabbana uses a complex anti-counterfeiting system that includes a certificate of authenticity, a heat-impressed hologram, and a safety seal made with thread that reacts to ultraviolet light.

When all else fails, companies take legal action, going after the counterfeiters themselves and the retailers and websites that carry fake products. In 2004 alone, the luxury conglomerate LVMH spent $20 million to battle the black market, conducting more than six thousand raids and more than eight thousand legal actions worldwide.[19]

In sum, fashion brands do a lot to avoid piracy. Because they think it is bad for their business.

But could counterfeiting actually be a good thing? Might brands actually benefit from the existence of fakes?

When two law professors looked into this question, they found that the answer was counterintuitively yes.[20] And the reason had everything to do with identity signaling.

People, particularly fashion-conscious ones, care about what their clothes communicate about them. They want to be in fashion, or at least not wear something out of style.

But, if the signal value of styles never changed, people would never need to buy anything new. They could just keep wearing the same Ugg boots or skinny ties year after year. If Ugg boots and skinny ties always signaled cool, people would have no reason to exchange those items for something else. People could keep wearing the same stuff until it wore out.

This arrangement might make most consumers happy, but retailers and manufacturers probably wouldn't feel the same way. Revenues would drop and jobs would be lost.

Enter counterfeiters to save the day.

By making and distributing knockoffs, piracy speeds obsolescence. Inferior copies may tarnish the original article, but, by broadening availability, counterfeits also change what it means to wear a style or brand. If anyone can buy what looks like this season's Louis Vuitton bag, then the signal sent by carrying the bag erodes. As the discount prices allow the bag to diffuse widely, it no longer signals exclusive or trendsetter. Instead it comes to signal mass market or fashion follower. And, as a result, true fashionistas diverge and buy something new.

Language works the same way. Teenagers start using words like "yolo" or "dip." Eventually their parents adopt the phrases to seem cool or hip. But adoption by outsiders changes the meaning. What once signaled cool starts to signal trying too hard. So teens abandon the phrase. And by the time Grandma starts saying she's ready to dip out from Thanksgiving dinner, everyone has moved on to something else.

Companies want to show they're ahead of the curve, so they glom on to management styles like Six Sigma and total quality management. Big or successful companies breed imitators, so smaller firms start copying anything they see "innovative" firms doing. But once enough imitators have copied, these approaches lose their value as signals that the firm is a pioneer. So firms that want to stand out have to move on.

Consequently, identity-signaling drives things to both catch on and die out. Some small set of early adopters start saying a particular phrase or using a particular management practice. If the early adopters are seen as cool, innovative, or desirable, others imitate them to try to signal the desired identity. And as more and more people flood in, the phrase, management practice, or other cultural item catches on and starts to become popular.

But once these later adopters jump in, the signal starts to change. What once was a signal of being cool or innovative starts to shift and signal something else. So the early adopters abandon the item to avoid signaling an undesired identity. Which only speeds up the signal change. Eventually, even the later adopters abandon the item as the original desired meaning has been lost. What was once popular is now the opposite.

Fashion cycles happen often, but counterfeiting helps speed the process. By ensuring its distribution, counterfeiting encourages fashions to die. But in so doing, piracy keeps consumers clamoring for new ones. As Shakespeare once quipped, "The fashion wears out more apparel than the man."

PUTTING SOCIAL INFLUENCE TO WORK

While minority students avoiding achievement or people not getting medical care because of signaling concerns is disheartening, the silver lining is that these same concepts, when applied correctly, can be used to encourage good decisions.

Public service announcements, particularly in the health domain, often focus on information. Antismoking ads talk about the negative health effects of lighting up, and antidrug campaigns encourage parents to "talk to your kids about the dangers of drugs." The notion is that information will change people's minds. Tell people about the negative consequences of smoking, drugs, or unhealthy eating, and they'll come around and do the right thing.

Unfortunately, more information doesn't always lead to better decisions. Teens who smoke know about the risks, but they do it anyway. Kids know that candy and chips are bad for them, but that still doesn't change their behavior.

Associating desired behaviors with aspiration groups, or desired identities, is often more effective. Popeye always ate spinach to make himself strong, and this association is believed to have boosted U.S. spinach consumption by a third.[21] Advertisers have long recognized this, linking stars like Michael Jordan with everything from shoes to food to soft drinks. Want to be like Mike? This product will help. If someone people idolize is doing something, they'll want to do it as well.*

Undesired identities can be equally effective. Binge drinking is a huge problem on college campuses. Students often drink more

---

* Children may not realize that Wonder Woman gets her power from cauliflower, or that the sports star they emulate loves beets, but sharing the news will increase kids' consumption of vegetables and other healthy foods. One parent convinced their two young boys that broccoli looked like a dinosaur tree, and that by eating broccoli they could pretend they were long-necked dinosaurs. The dinosaur-loving kids thought that was pretty cool and told their friends, and soon their whole day care group loved broccoli. See Brian Wansink's great book, *Mindless Eating: Why We Eat More Than We Think* (New York: Bantam, 2007).

than they should, resulting in a variety of accidents and health issues.

To try and combat this problem, behavioral scientist Lindsay Rand and I shifted the identity some students associated with drinking.[22] We went to college dormitories and put up posters featuring a geeky-looking guy (a cross between a hip-hop wannabe frat guy and the skipper from *Gilligan's Island*) holding a drink. The posters reminded students to "think when you drink, no one wants to be mistaken for this guy." By linking binge drinking to an identity students did not want to be associated with, we hoped to shift their behavior.

And it worked. Compared to other students shown posters with traditional information-based appeals (e.g., 1,700 college students die each year from alcohol related injuries, so "think when you drink, your health is important"), students who saw the posters linking binge drinking to an undesired identity reported drinking 50 percent less alcohol.

We used the same idea to get people to eat healthier. We approached patrons at a local restaurant and reminded some of them that a group they tended not to want to look like consumed a lot of junk food. People chose healthy salads instead of greasy burgers when junk food was associated with an identity they didn't want to signal. Shifting the signal helped health

Similar identity-based interventions can be beneficial in a variety of contexts. When speaking about the negative effects of "acting white," President Obama said that America needed to "eradicate the slander that says a black youth with a book is acting white."

But changing the stereotype requires more than just changing what people say. It requires shifting the identity associated with academic achievement to one that more clearly features minority students.

In predominantly African-American schools, the negative link between academic achievement and social status is naturally weaker. Because most of the best-performing students in these schools are African-American, it diffuses any notion that doing well is acting white. Seeing black student after black student doing well makes it hard to think that doing well is a white thing.

Well-designed programs can also shift these signals. In the case of women and science, technology, engineering, and math, it can be as simple as slightly changing the environment. Women were much more interested in enrolling in a computer class when the classroom was decorated with general-interest magazines, plants, and other neutral décor (rather than stereotypically male things like *Star Wars* posters and science fiction books) or when they interacted with a computer science major who wore regular clothes (rather than a shirt that said I CODE, THEREFORE I AM). The neutral environment or nonstereotypical interaction partner increased women's sense of belonging, making them feel like they fit in.[23] Drawing attention to academically successful minority students, particularly those who are seen as popular, should have similar effects for race. The identity associated with a particular behavior or action is often just as important as the more "functional" value it provides.[24]

Stigma-associated signals are particularly important for understanding health risk perception. The more susceptible people think they are to a disease, the more likely they are to get tested and change their behavior. Yet adding a stigmatized reason (e.g., unprotected sex) to a list of potential ways to catch a disease makes people paradoxically *less* likely to think they could have contracted the disease and less likely to get tested. Compared to people who were told the disease could be contracted in three non-stigmatized ways (e.g., exposure to a crowd), adding a stigmatized way to the list made people 60 percent less likely to think they were at risk for the disease. Adding an additional way to contract the disease should only *increase* risk of exposure (there are now more ways to get it), yet people felt less comfortable admitting vulnerability because the added cause carried stigma.[25]

More generally, managing identity signals is key for making sure something not only catches on, but stays popular. If people are supporting a cause or buying a product because they like what it communicates about them, advocacy and sales can increase exponentially as people rush to jump on the bandwagon.

But things can come crashing down just as quickly. What was cool today may be passé tomorrow as people move on to the next hot issue or item.

British luxury brand Burberry faced just this issue. While the brand had upscale roots among greying executives who love to golf, by the early 2000s, the meaning had shifted. Burberry's distinctive camel check pattern had become the uniform de rigueur for "chavs," or white working-class soccer hooligans with a penchant for the bottle. Taxi drivers would refuse to pick up men in Burberry baseball caps, and by the time a drug-abusing soap actress, her daughter, and the daughter's stroller appeared draped in the pattern, Burberry's original patrons had fled to other brands.

To restore Burberry's luster, new CEO Angela Ahrendts not only cracked down on counterfeiters, she toned down the check. Ahrendts removed the iconic plaid pattern from 90 percent of the product line. When the checkered pattern did appear, it appeared on the inside of coats rather than splashed all over the outside.

And the strategy worked. Earnings soared and the company reclaimed their identity. By making the branding less prominent, Burberry maintained its high-quality status, but shook off any hangers-on who only wanted the brand for what it signaled.

Another solution is to offer multiple product lines. Lots of families own a Toyota Camry because it is a safe, reliable car. But families driving it may turn other consumers off. If you just got a big promotion at work and want to show people you've made it, buying a car that signals suburban dad isn't going to cut it.

So Toyota created Lexus. The Lexus brand has a more luxurious feel and offers higher-end cars at a higher price point. Part of this is about appealing to customers who want something fancier than a Camry. But part of it is also about identity. Lexus offers people who might have driven something like a Camry a way to distinguish themselves from the families in their Camrys. A way to move up, but not out of the Toyota brand.

Scion, another Toyota brand, does something similar for younger consumers who like to customize their rides. The cars themselves offer different features, but the symbolic offering is different as well. Driving a Scion signals something quite different from driving a Toyota, and the multiple sub-brands allows Toyota to retain these different segments by offering desired, albeit different, signals to each of them.

Meaning can also be managed by evoking broader identities. Republicans are wary of supporting a liberal cause and Democrats feel similarly about conservative ones. But framing something as a human rights issue helps it rise above partisan lines. This superordinate, or higher-level, identity is something more people can buy into. And because it evokes a broader identity, it's less likely that people will avoid it.

So far we've talked about two ways social influence impacts behavior: imitation and differentiation. People can do the same thing as others or do something different. But there is a third route as well. Doing both at the same time.

4. Similar but Different

Twice a year, a secret meeting takes place somewhere in Europe. Representatives from various countries gather in a sparse room in an undisclosed location, debating for days until a decision is reached. Presentations are made, arguments volleyed, and sides taken.

It's not a nuclear security meeting, or a G8 summit, but an event that some might argue has a bigger impact on our everyday life. The meeting to decide the Color of the Year.

Since 1999, the prophets of color have met to anoint the shade that will rule runways and aisles for the next twelve months.

In 2014, it was color number 18-3224, otherwise known as Radiant Orchid. This vibrant shade of purple contains hints of pink, and was lauded for its ability to encourage "expanded creativity and originality."

In 2013, the Color of the Year was Emerald, a lush green that signified well-being, balance, and harmony. These popular hues were preceded in prior years by colors such as Turquoise, Honeysuckle, and Tangerine Tango.

Pantone, a cross-industry color company that provides a reference guide for thousands of colors in a standardized format, convenes the meeting. Before the meeting, Pantone surveys manufacturers, retailers, and designers around the world to understand what colors they plan to use in the next year and what colors they see bubbling up around them. These insights are then organized, filtered, and debated by the attendees, with the results summarized in *Pantoneview*, a $750 publication purchased by everyone from Gap and Estée Lauder to package designers and the floral industry.*

These companies hope to decode what color will be hot next year. It's tough enough to figure out whether boot-cut or skinny jeans will be popular, or whether flower buyers will be drawn to tulips or roses. But color adds even more complexity. Will consumers want purple tulips or red ones? Will grey jeans sell well or is black a safer bet?

Given the long lead times for producing products, color decisions need to be made months in advance. Farmers have to plant

---

* Picking the right colors to produce involves a bit of game theory. Most companies would prefer to be on trend rather than off it, but each company's decision about what to produce not only responds to the trend, it helps shape it. What they produce affects what consumers buy and thus what becomes popular. There's also safety in numbers: if many companies across industries rally around the same colors in a given year, those colors are more likely to be popular, and sales will be high. So Pantone's color forecast provides a valuable coordinating mechanism. By following the same source, companies try to insure themselves against picking the wrong color, going with lime green when everyone else goes orange.

It's also unclear whether Pantone's predictions merely reflect what is going on already or influence what becomes popular. Pantone may be an early detection system for a wave that is about to come in, but it may also be enough of a stimulus to start a wave in the first place.

the right bulbs and factories have to order the right thread. And no one wants to be forced to discount stacks of unsold inventory at the end of the season.

But while betting on the right colors is vital, it's also hard for any one company or designer to guess what color will be popular. Each business gets only a tiny slice of the full information pie. They see what people are buying in a small set of product categories in a small set of countries.

So companies look to Pantone to help them make educated guesses. Pantone collects a wide range of data from across the globe and provides a centralized, (hopefully) unbiased perspective. They give companies a broad sense of what is going on now, and what might be happening next. Predictions about which colors will be popular in the future.

If you look at the Colors of the Year over time, though, you notice an intriguing pattern. The year 2012's color, Tangerine Tango, looks strikingly similar to Tigerlily, a previous Color of the Year winner. And unless you squint, 2010's color, Turquoise, is a dead ringer for Blue Turquoise, the Color of the Year from a few years before.

Might there be some structure to cultural evolution? Could what's popular now shape what becomes popular next?

PREDICTING THE NEXT BIG THING

Hits happen in all sorts of industries. There are blockbuster movies, unicorn start-ups, and platinum albums. The *Fifty Shades of Grey* trilogy has sold over 125 million copies. Greek yogurt came out of nowhere to become one of the hottest foods in the United States.

Not surprisingly, predicting cultural trends is of huge interest to companies, consumers, and cultural critics alike. Will a new book be a hit or a flop? Will a particular public policy initiative catch on or fizzle fast? There are big rewards in being able to forecast success.

To get a leg up, companies build complex algorithms to try to predict whether a given product or song is catchy enough. So-called trend forecasters swirl the tea leaves and try to guess what will happen next.

But predicting the future is notoriously hard to do. As we know from the story of J. K. Rowling, even so-called "experts" have trouble identifying hits before they take off. For every "futurist" who prophesied the organic food movement, fifteen others predicted that "mechanized hugging booths" would be the wave of the future.

As the music research illustrated, people's tendency to follow others makes success volatile. Forecasting how popular a song, food, or even color will be seems almost impossible. Why some things succeed and others fail often seems random.

But might it be less random than it seems?

To find out, Wharton professor Eric Bradlow and statisticians Alex Braunstein and Yao Zhang and I decided to examine a domain that everyone knows at least something about.[1] First names.

Cesar had been hoping for a boy. Praying, actually. Sometimes twice a day. He and his wife, Rebecca, already had twin four-year-old girls, and there was only so much pink he could take. Sure, the girls played soccer and piano in addition to taking ballet lessons, but it would be nice to have another guy in the house. Another Y chromosome to balance out all the Xs.

So he did everything he could to make it happen. He started

with the easy stuff. Picking out shades of blue for the baby's room and wearing boxers rather than briefs.

Soon he began following all sorts of pseudoscience recommendations. He drank more coffee and encouraged Rebecca to eat "boy" foods like red meat, fish, and pasta. He consulted a Chinese gender chart to help them decide when to conceive and asked Rebecca to drink cough syrup with guaifenesin to loosen mucus (don't even ask). He even tried consulting a psychic.

It was a harrowing first four and a half months.

Eventually, they went in for an ultrasound. They stared at the pictures, looking for any hint of the gender.

Then, the doctor uttered the words Cesar had been waiting for. It would be a boy.

Cesar and the girls were ecstatic. There would be another boy in the house. But then came the tougher decision. What to name him.

Rebecca came up with a long list of possibilities: Eli, Julian, and Michael. Jason, Daniel, and Liam. Gavan and James and Holden and Tucker.

She had been a teacher before becoming pregnant with the girls, so every name had an association. Gabriel sounded nice enough, but one of the worst kids she ever taught was a Gabriel, so that was out. Holden was fine but there were too many running around school the past few years.

The name also had to fit with the baby's sisters' names, Parker and Allie. Something that had a comparable feel. A similar number of syllables and a little more new sounding than traditional.

Each time they thought they had reached a solution, someone close to them would shoot it down. "'Michael' sounds too old-fashioned," Rebecca's mom complained. "'Liam' sounds too new-agey," a relative grumbled. From then on, they kept all new ideas to themselves.

Finally, in early 2006, Keegan was born.

Names, like other words, can be broken up into a series of basic sound parts called phonemes. Each phoneme stands for a perceptually distinct unit of sound in a particular language. Take the name Jake. It starts with a /j/ (as in words like "joy" and "jam"). Next comes an /ā/ sound ("ay" as in "lay" and "make") and it ends with a /k/ (as in "take" and "bake").

Phonemes may seem like letters, but there are some important differences. There are only twenty-six letters in the English language, but over forty phonemes, in part because the same letter can make different sounds in different words.

Try saying words like "cat" and "laugh" a couple times. In both words, the letter *a* makes an "ahh" sound.

Now trying saying words like "Jake" and "maid." Same letter *a*, but here it sounds more like "ay" than "ahh."

Something similar happens with the letter *e*. In words like "end" and "friend" the letter *e* makes an "eh" sound, while in words like "be" and "key" it makes an "ee" sound. In the name Jake the *e* is silent.

Different letters can sometimes even make the same sounds. In words like "kit" and "rack" the letter *k* makes the "k" sound, while in words like "cat" and "car" the letter *c* is making that same sound. Try switching the *c* in "cat" to a *k* (i.e., "kat" as in Kit Kat) and the word still sounds pretty much identical.

The name Keegan is six letters long, but it is composed of only five phonemes. It starts with a hard /k/ (as in "kick" and "kaleidoscope"), then moves to an /ē/ sound ("ee" as in "feet" and "leech"), followed by a /g/ (as in "gas" and "gill"), an /a/ sound ("ah" as in "fat" or "hat"), and ending with an /n/ (as in the name Nancy or "nice").

For Rebecca and Cesar, Keegan was the perfect name. It hit all the requirements. Strong sounding but not too long. Modern enough but not obviously so. Close enough to Rebecca's maiden name to pass the family lineage along.

When Keegan got to kindergarten, though, his teacher noticed something unusual. There wasn't another Keegan in class, but there were an awful lot of kids whose names sounded similar. Going through the class list there was Keegan, Kevin, Kimberly, Keely, Carson, and Carmen. Out of twenty kids, six had names that either began with *K* or started with a hard-*K* sound. Why did so many children have similar-sounding names?

The answer, it turns out, was Hurricane Katrina.

What's in a name? From Emily and Eric to Apple and Blue Ivy, everyone has one. Our names not only follow us our entire lives, they also influence the lives we lead. First names affect everything from how attractive people seem to whether they receive callbacks from potential employers.[2]

So it's no surprise that parents agonize over the right moniker for their child. Prospective mothers and fathers spend hours searching through naming books, combing through blogs, and vetting possibilities.

But what makes a particular name sound, well, good?

Associations clearly matter. Just as Rebecca avoided Gabriel because it reminded her of someone she didn't like, the particular person a name conjures can have a big impact on choice. That Eva sounds old-fashioned can be good or bad depending on your preferences. Parents avoid names like Adolf for obvious reasons.

But when we analyzed how the popularity of different names changed over time, we found something interesting.

Through their role in providing social security numbers, the U.S. Social Security Administration keeps track of what names parents give to their kids. For over 125 years, they have records of how many people with different names were born each year. How many Jacobs and Susans and Kyles and Jessies were born in 1900, 1901, 1902, and so on. More than 280 million births and over seven thousand different names.

Some names (like Luke and Mia) have become more popular over time, while others (such as Charles and Elizabeth) have become less popular. Some names (Paula or Tess) increased in popularity for a period, only to decrease again. And some names (Jack or Laura) peaked twice, increasing and decreasing and increasing and decreasing again.

When we sifted through all the data, we found that hurricanes influenced how people named their children. Following Hurricane Katrina in 2005, for example, almost 10 percent more babies were born with names beginning with a K sound (compared to the prior year). After Hurricane Andrew in 1992, names that started with a soft "ah" sound increased 7 percent. That's thousands of babies getting certain names, just because a big hurricane happened to hit.

On the surface, this doesn't make sense. Why would anyone name his child after a hurricane?

Hurricane Katrina was one of the five deadliest hurricanes in the history of the United States. It caused more than $100 billion in property damage and killed more than 1,800 people.[3] Who would want their child associated with such a lethal natural disaster? It would be like naming your son Stalin and hoping no one made the connection.

This intuition is partially right. Popularity of the name Katrina itself decreased by almost 40 percent after the storm hit. The first association most people had with the name Katrina right after the hurricane occurred was the storm itself, so many people shied away from giving that name to their kids.*

But that wasn't the only effect Hurricane Katrina had on naming patterns. While the hurricane decreased the popularity of the name Katrina *itself*, it increased the popularity of *other* names that began with the same phoneme or hard *K* sound. Use of the name Keely increased by 25 percent. Fifty-five percent more babies were given the name Kaelyn. And names like Kinsey, Kate, Carmine, and Cora all became more popular.

And the reason has everything to do with the value of moderate similarity.

When picking a name, parents think a lot about how popular the name is. While some parents like unique names (Moxie Crimefighter, anyone?), most want a name that is a little more, well, standard. Too popular, though, and people may avoid it.

---

* In some cases, though, the popularity of the hurricane's name actually increases after the hurricane hits. If few people tend to think of the name, even the negative attention to that name might increase its popularity by making the name more at the top-of-mind. Prior research my colleagues and I have done on negative publicity shows exactly that. Getting a negative review can actually increase the sales of a book if that book was not well-known prior to the review.

But beyond the name itself, what about the popularity of *other* names?

Sure, lots of baby Keegans running around might affect whether parents choose that name, but what about baby Kevins and Calebs? Could the fact that these names start with the same hard *K* sound affect whether parents decide to name their boy Keegan?

It turns out that the answer is yes. Names are more likely to be popular when similar-sounding names have been popular recently.

People are more likely to name their children Morgan or Maggie when there are more baby Michaels and Madisons. And more likely to name their kids Lisa or Lyle if Lexi and Lance have been popular recently.

Hurricanes have a similar influence on naming patterns because they influence how often we hear certain names, and thus sounds.

When a particularly damaging storm like Katrina hits, people hear the name Katrina again and again. The nightly news talks about when Katrina will make landfall, people at the grocery store are chatting about how much havoc Katrina has wreaked on the country. Again, and again, people hear the name Katrina and the sounds that make up that name. And while this echo chamber drives parents to avoid the name Katrina itself, it also leads them to give their babies similar-sounding names.

Analogous patterns occur in a variety of domains.

Some cars look more prototypical, or similar to other cars on the market. The Volkswagen Jetta, for example, looks a lot like many other cars out there. It has the same standard-looking grille and lightly sloping headlights. One could easily confuse it with a Toyota, Nissan, or a number of other available options.

Other cars look more different. The Volkswagen Beetle looks unlike anything else on the market. It has round bug eyes, a dome-shaped roof, and a grille that almost smiles at you when you look at it head-on. It's actually built on the same chassis as the normal-looking Volkswagen Golf and has the same technology, but its appearance is quite distinct.

These differences in visual appearance predict sales. Whether looking at economy or more premium cars, and even controlling for things like price and advertising, models that look more prototypical, or similar to other cars on the market, sell better.[4]

Similarity increases evaluation (and sales) for the same reason that mere exposure works. Just as the more we see something, the more we like it, the more we see something, the more we like *other* things that share similar features.

Imagine you're asked to participate in an experiment regarding how quickly people can make judgments of new or novel shapes.

You'll be shown a number of drawings, presented at rapid speeds. After a drawing is flashed briefly, it will be replaced by a background of black, white, and grey dots. The background will give you a place to focus your eyes before the next picture is flashed. The pictures will be flashed so quickly that they may be difficult to see, but do your best.[5]

The first drawing you see is something like the following:

It's actually a Chinese character, but your job is not to guess what it means, just to answer how much you like it. (If you happen to speak Mandarin, just focus on the shape's visual appeal.)

On a scale from 1 to 100, where 1 means you don't like it at all and 100 means you like it quite a bit, how much do you like the drawing?

You only get to look at the image for 5 milliseconds, or approximately a honeybee's wing flap, before being shown something like this background picture to cleanse your visual palate:

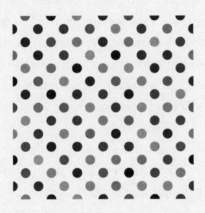

Then, just a second later, you're shown another drawing. How much do you like this one?

社会

The drawings are shown so rapidly that you don't have time to process them in depth. They just seem like abstract shapes whizzing by.

After seeing a number of these drawings, you move on to

the second phase of the experiment. Here you are again shown drawings, but now they show up for slightly longer, around one second.

How much do you like this one?

传染

Without your realizing it, the drawings in the second part of the experiment are a mixture of three types of shapes. Some of the drawings are Chinese characters you were shown during the initial phase. They went by too fast for you to realize you've seen them before, but they are repeats all the same.

Another group of drawings are novel Chinese characters. They have the same structure as the first set, but you weren't shown them in the initial phase.

The third group is made up of random polygons. Multisided shapes like a rhombus or a pentagon.

Thus some of the shapes are old (the Chinese characters you've seen), some are new but similar (the Chinese characters you haven't seen), and some are new but different (the polygons).

When scientists conducted a similar experiment, they found two things. First, exposure influenced liking. People liked shapes they had seen previously, even though they didn't realize they'd seen them. And they liked those previously seen shapes more than the random polygons they hadn't seen before. Just like the women in the psychology class over the course of the semester, the more you see something, the more you like it.

More remarkably, this boost in evaluation also spread to the new but similar items. Seeing one set of Chinese characters made people like other Chinese characters more, even if they hadn't seen those specific characters previously.

And it wasn't just something weird about Chinese characters. The researchers found the same results if the initial shapes shown were random polygons instead. Seeing one set of polygons not only made participants like those polygons more, it made them like other polygons that they hadn't even seen.

The more you see something, the more you like *similar* things as well.

Part of the reason similar things look or sound better is familiarity. If you've seen something before, it's easier for your brain to process. The mind doesn't have to do as much work to figure out what it is, and this reduced effort generates a positive feeling that we interpret as familiarity.

The lure of the familiar has evolutionary benefits. It helps children bond with their caregivers, guides animals toward plants that are safe to eat, and helps spouses stay together through mood swings, dirty clothes on the floor, and other bumps in the road.

Imagine every time you encountered something, you had to figure out if it was safe. Whether it is good or bad, positive or negative. Is that person in your house your spouse or someone trying to rob you? Is that thing in the fridge safe to eat or poisonous?

Simple actions we don't even code as decisions would become arduous. Eating cornflakes for breakfast wouldn't just be habit, it would be a life life-and-death decision. You'd have to pop one flake in your mouth, and then wait to see what happened before eating any more.

Humans and other animals evolved a mechanism that reduces

this effort. If we've encountered something before, particularly recently, it becomes easier to process. Whether it's a person, food, or kitchen utensil, less work is needed to figure out what it is.

This ease of processing, in turn, is coded positively. It's the warm glow of familiarity.

Importantly, this warm glow doesn't just affect things we've actually been exposed to. It also extends to things that share features with what we've seen or heard previously.

Someone who looks like someone you know seems more familiar because they have a similar haircut or facial structure.[6] Keegan sounds better when you've heard the name Katrina a lot recently because they start with the same hard *K* sound. These things look or sound familiar because they share common features with what we've seen or heard before.

This liking of similar things helps us deal with the variation that permeates everyday life. People don't look exactly the same every time we see them, and neither does food. Someone may wear a different shirt or style their hair a different way.

So, for a "seen-before" decoder to be useful, it has to be able to handle that variation. Even if the person we saw this week doesn't look exactly like the best friend we saw last month, we need to be able to code both of them as familiar. Otherwise each time we saw something would be like seeing it for the first time.

Liking similar things is also useful from an inference perspective. If you've eaten a certain berry one hundred times and never gotten sick, it's likely that a similar-looking berry is safe as well. If you've interacted with someone one hundred times and they've always been nice to you, it's likely that someone who looks similar (and thus might be related) might also be friendly. Liking similar things thus provides another shortcut to judgment that makes life easier.

Familiarity, though, is only part of the story.

SOMETHING OLD, SOMETHING NEW

Every so often, pollsters conduct surveys to rank U.S. presidents. Companies or media outlets compile data from academic historians, political scientists, and public opinion to see who had the most positive effect on the country. Just as *Consumer Reports* might rank car seats, these surveys weigh achievements and leadership qualities, as well as faults and failures, and spit out a ranking of the best and the worst presidents (or at least good and less good).

Dozens of high-profile rankings have been performed over the past fifty years, but certain names often bubble to the top. Famous presidents such as George Washington, Thomas Jefferson, and Abraham Lincoln consistently rank high on the list. Along with Franklin D. Roosevelt and Theodore Roosevelt, these high-achieving leaders had a significant influence on the course of history.

John F. Kennedy, Ronald Reagan, and Bill Clinton also often do well. These presidents did well in public opinion polls, even if they don't rank as highly among presidential scholars.

The bottom of the list often includes names like Warren G. Harding and James Buchanan. Harding appointed campaign contributors and allies to prominent political positions that they milked for personal gain. Buchanan did little to impede the spread of slavery or the growing unrest that eventually became the Confederacy.

Between the best and the worst are names that have faded

over time. Presidents that have not been completely forgotten, but had neither the positive impact of a Lincoln nor the negative scandals of a Nixon to remain at the top of public consciousness.

One such president was Calvin Coolidge.

Born in Plymouth Notch, Vermont, on July 4, 1872, Coolidge is the only president to be born on Independence Day. A lawyer by trade, he worked his way through Massachusetts state politics, becoming a state legislator and eventually governor. He was elected vice president in 1920 and became president after the sudden death of Warren G. Harding in 1923.

Known as a small-government conservative, Coolidge restored confidence in the presidency after Harding's scandals. Still, he never had the influence of some of the men that preceded or followed him. He said little—he was known as "Silent Cal"—and his legacy is divided between people who favored his reductions in government programs and opponents who thought government should play a more active role in regulating and directing the economy.

Though his term in office may not have been that memorable, Coolidge's name is forever linked to a fundamental aspect of human behavior. Legend has it that the president and his wife, Grace, once visited a government farm. As much as Calvin Coolidge was shy, Grace was outgoing, and was a popular hostess at the White House.

After arriving at the farm, the two went on separate tours of the facility. When Mrs. Coolidge passed a set of pens housing chickens, she stopped to ask the person in charge how frequently the rooster copulated. "Dozens of times a day," the man responded.

"Please tell that to the President," Mrs. Coolidge requested.

Later that day, Mr. Coolidge himself walked by the pens. He was informed about the roosters' behavior as well as his wife's comment.

"Same hen every time?" the president asked the keeper.

"Oh, no, Mr. President, a different one each time."

The president thought to himself for a moment and nodded. "Tell that to Mrs. Coolidge."[7]

Variety, the saying goes, is the spice of life. If we just liked what was familiar, there would be no reason not to pick the same thing again and again. Nothing should be more familiar than doing what we did before. Eating the same meal for lunch, wearing the same clothes to work, and going to the same place for vacation.

Decisions would be easy because there would often be no decisions at all. We'd just do what we've done before.

But while picking the same thing over and over would make life easy, it's easy to see that most people would hate it.

While familiarity is good, people also have a competing drive for novelty.[8] Humans have an innate preference for stimulation: what's fresh, original, or unexperienced.

Sure, eating the same ham-and-cheese sandwich every day is safe and familiar, but most people relish the opportunity to occasionally try something new. To branch out and experience something different. Ham and cheese is good, but how about a little mustard? Or a different type of bread? Actually, while we're at it, the new wrap place that opened up down the block looks intriguing, why not check it out? Who knows, hummus and sprouts might be worth a try.

Trying new things allows us to acquire useful information.

You might think strawberry is your favorite flavor of ice cream, but if you've never tried anything else, it's hard to know for sure.

So, once in a while we poke our heads out of our tentative turtle shells and try something different. We get chocolate, pistachio, or even something wild like tutti-frutti or bacon-flavored ice cream.

Will we like bacon better than strawberry? Probably not. But by trying new flavors we learn something about our preferences. Bacon might not tantalize our taste buds, but we might like pistachio better than strawberry, and without trying something new we never would have known.

Novelty has a host of benefits.[9] Doing new activities once in a while (say, taking a pottery class or going to a museum) boosts life satisfaction and doing novel activities with a relationship partner makes people more satisfied in their relationship. Novel news articles are more likely to garner attention, and changes to the workplace tend to increase productivity.

One of the most studied aspects of novelty, though, is the so-called Coolidge effect, named after the experience the president and his wife had at the farm.[10]

As anyone who has ever had hamsters can attest, the little guys love to mate. Some hamsters start reproducing as young as four to five weeks old, and can have several litters a year.

Hamsters will even mate multiple times in one sitting. Some males will mate with the same female five or even ten times in a row. Mating attempts will continue until the male is exhausted and no longer interested in mating further. The female might poke and prod the male, but he's done.

Researchers, though, wondered whether animals' drive for novelty would be enough to overcome this apparent exhaustion.[11]

The male hamster seems sated, uninterested in further action. But what would happen if a new female is introduced?

Sure enough, while the male seemed exhausted, a new potential sexual partner was enough to perk him back up. When a novel female appeared, the male's sexual interest was reignited.

This same pattern has been observed in a number of mammals. Rats, cattle, even voles, show the same sexual behavior. Some female animals show similar effects, albeit less strong. Just like the rooster who copulated multiple times a day when different hens were introduced, for the hamster, novelty was the spice of love.

So which is it? Do people like familiar things or do they like novel ones?

THE GOLDILOCKS EFFECT

Think about the first time you experience something new. Imagine you've come home from a business trip and you walk into the living room to find that your spouse bought a new piece of furniture. "It was time for a change, honey, and this ottoman was on sale, so I snapped it up."

Or you walk into the bathroom to find that all the old towels have been swapped out for new ones. "The old grey ones were getting so ratty, so I got us some great plush turquoise replacements. Don't they look great?"

How would you feel the moment you saw the towels? The first few milliseconds they entered your field of view?

Your first reaction would probably be a slightly aversive surprise. You liked the old towels, and while they were getting a little frayed at the edges, these new towels are so . . . well, new. They stand out like a misplaced note on the clarinet. The new towels make the bathroom feel weird and foreign, a different place from what you are used to. Like you ended up in the neighbors' bathroom rather than your own.

Novelty, at least at first, often evokes a mildly negative reaction. Because they are new, novel things require additional processing and attention. We have to figure out whether they are okay, whether they are safe. Our curiosity is piqued, but we also get a little anxious. Novelty can be scary. Even if the new thing is just a couple of turquoise towels.

Will they work as well as the old ones? Will they be as cozy? Until we've had the chance to use them a couple of times, we're just not sure.

Through repeated exposure, however, things that were once novel start to become more familiar. We use the new towels a couple times and slowly we start to like them. They're just as comfy as the old towels and they have a nice way of brightening up the bathroom on a dreary day.

The towels are no longer alien, they've become part of our routine. After a couple weeks we don't even notice them anymore.

Too many exposures to the same thing, though, and we start to get bored. The towels start to look dull, the same recipe gets tiresome, and the movie is no longer engaging the third time we watch it. What was once positively familiar becomes humdrum and monotonous.

The more complex the stimulus, the less likely the habituation. So while we may tire of hearing the same song or eating the same cereal relatively quickly, we're less likely to get bored of our spouse or a restaurant. The latter are more varied experiences that often change each time we experience them. While the song stays relatively the same, our spouse says different things and looks different each time we see them, so it doesn't feel like we're experiencing the same thing each time. As a result, while relatively simple things may have quick appeal but soon become boring, relatively complex things may take longer to warm to, but also have a longer-lasting appeal.

How concentrated the interactions are also matters. Hearing the same song ten times in a row gets quite tedious, but hear it once a week over ten weeks and it doesn't get as tiresome. The more time there is between interactions, the more novel the experience seems, and the more we like it.

Personal control is also important. Most things never reach the point where they become tiresome because people choose to stop consuming them before then. If we find ourselves starting to get bored of a certain recipe, we stop making it for a while. If we tire of a restaurant, we go someplace else for a few months until we feel like going again. Thus we never get to the point where our positive feelings start to turn negative.

In some ways, our emotional reactions are a bit like Goldilocks from Goldilocks and the Three Bears. In the children's tale, each of the bears has its own preference for bedding and food. One bear has a firm bed, one bear has a soft bed, and one has a bed somewhere in the middle. One bear likes its porridge hot, one likes it cold, and one likes it somewhere in between.

Goldilocks tries each, but is always turned off by the extremes. The firm bed is too firm and the soft bed too soft. The hot porridge too hot and the cold porridge too cold. But the middle bed and the middle porridge? Well, those are just right.

Affective reactions often follow a similar Goldilocks effect, or inverted-U-shape trajectory. When something is new, we initially feel slightly negatively (or neutral). Then, after repeated exposure, things become more familiar and we start to feel more positively. But eventually, after too many exposures, boredom kicks in and liking declines.[12]

Too novel and it's unfamiliar. Too familiar and it's boring. But in between and it's just right.

When British psychologists examined how much people liked different last names, for example, they found just this pattern.[13] Students were asked to consider sixty different surnames, randomly selected from the telephone directory. Half the students rated how much they liked the different last names, while the other half rated how familiar the names were.

Very unfamiliar names, such as Baskin, Nall, and Bodle, weren't liked that much. At the other end of the spectrum, highly familiar names such as Smith and Brown were also disliked. So what did people like?

Turns out the names people liked the most were the ones that fell in the middle. Names like Shelley or Cassell that were moderately familiar (at least to Brits). Right between unfamiliar and too familiar was just right.

Familiarity and novelty can also be mixed in the same item. Some elements of a song (a chord progression or singer's voice) may be familiar, while others (the lyrics) are new. A new recipe for turkey chili takes something you've made many times before (chili) and puts a novel spin on it. Just like similar sounding names, these variations on a theme increase liking.

Moderately discrepant things also tend to garner more attention.[14] Take an infant who has just learned a set of expectations about what a dog looks like. How many legs a dog has, that it has fur, and a range of typical sizes.

Seeing a dog picture they've seen before is less interesting because it is wholly familiar, and seeing something that looks completely different from a dog (a whale, for example) should be so unfamiliar as to be confusing and incomprehensible. But something that is moderately discrepant from their existing knowledge or expectations (a hairless dog) should be particularly intriguing because it doesn't fit with their existing notion of what a dog should be. It's similar enough to be comprehensible, but different enough to evoke interest and exploration.

The right blend of familiarity and novelty also drives what becomes popular. Classical music is more likely to be popular if the transitions between notes are somewhat similar to classical music in general, but different enough from music composed at that time.[15] High-impact scientific research is grounded in prior work with a sprinkling of unusual combinations of prior ideas.[16] And hit fashion styles, such as skinny jeans, often take something we all know well (jeans) and add novelty (a new cut).

Things that catch on, then, whether in music, fashion, or any other domain, often hit this Goldilocks range. Similar enough to what is already out there to evoke the warm glow of familiarity, but novel enough to seem new and not just derivative of what came before. Similarity shapes popularity because it makes novel things feel familiar.*

Returning to hurricanes and baby names, similar names have the benefit of being new and old at the same time. If Karen is a popular baby name this year, people may be all Karened out. The

---

* The warm glow of familiarity is most effective when we don't expect it. If we know why something feels familiar ("I just ate there last week"), that familiarity doesn't boost liking as much as if that familiarity in unexpected. This is part of the reason why similar things become popular. They feel familiar, but people can't immediately tell why.

name sounds too familiar, and no longer sounds unique, so next year's parents will move on to something else.

But as they pick amongst the other names out there, that Karen was popular may sway their choice. Similar names, like Katy or Darren, may sound better, even if the parents that pick them don't realize why.

OPTIMALLY DISTINCT

Sam, a junior at Princeton University, had just finished her political science homework, and was headed to dinner when she came across the table set out in front of the eating club. Someone was giving people Starbucks gift cards in exchange for filling out a quick survey. It seemed easy enough, and she had a couple minutes before her friends were supposed to show up for dinner, so she dove right in.

The first few questions were simple demographic information. Year in school, age, gender, and so on. The next question asked: Which of the following best describes your fashion style? Preppy, trendy, athletic, classic, edgy/rock, bohemian, indie/hipster, punk/skater, or other.

Sam hated being boxed in, and even after thinking about it for a minute, none of the categories seemed right. She checked the "other" box and wrote in "eclectic!"

One crisp fall evening a few years ago, I was taking the dog for a walk when I noticed two guys about a block in front of me. It was a Friday night, so there were lots of people going out to dinner, or grabbing drinks with friends, but these two guys stood out.

They had medium builds, and one was a few inches taller than the other, but they grabbed my attention because of what they were wearing. In addition to jeans, and some normal-looking sneakers, both were wearing shirts with horizontal brown stripes. Shirts reminiscent of old-fashioned prison garb (albeit in brown) or what you might look for in a *Where's Waldo?* book.

It's not unusual to see groups of friends dressing similarly. On a Friday night, one crew of guys might be wearing untucked button-downs or polo shirts while another group will wear V-neck T-shirts and jeans. One group of girls might be blousy tops and heels, while another will wear Ugg boots and hooded sweatshirts.

But while button-down shirts or Ugg boots are common, brown horizontally striped tops are a bit more rare. And it wasn't as if they were wearing the exact same thing. One guy had on a polo shirt and one had on a sweatshirt. But both had horizontal brown stripes, with either white or grey between them. Weird.

Were they on the way to some striped theme party I hadn't been invited to? Or might their fashion faux pas tell us something deeper about how social influence shapes behavior?

Professors Cindy Chan, Leaf Van Boven, and I decided to take a trip to Princeton University to find out.[17]

In 1853, Princeton University's trustees and faculty voted to ban fraternities and secret societies. The university was wary of how these groups divided the student body (in this pre–Civil War time period, groups often formed around opposing sides) and worried about the cliquishness they developed.

The ban in itself would not have been an issue, but combined with the lack of campus dining options, students were forced to begin to take their meals in boardinghouses around town. Options flourished. By 1876 there were over twenty such places that catered to the students. They became known as "eating clubs."

To this day, eating clubs are the center of social life at Princeton. While fraternities were reinstated in the 1980s, the few that exist remain unhoused, and only a small percentage of the students participate.

Instead, social life revolves around the eating clubs. Not only do most upperclassmen take their meals in the eating clubs, but many also go there to study, hang out, and play sports. Thursday and Saturday nights most of the eating clubs host parties, and different clubs have yearly events or concerts that cater to their members.

Given how important these clubs are, my colleagues and I wondered if which club people belonged to would influence how they dressed. Just like the two friends wearing brown-striped shirts, would students from the same club all dress in a "uniform" of sorts? And would these uniforms be distinct enough that observers could tell which club someone belonged to based on the clothes they was wearing?

We picked two popular eating clubs. The first was the Cottage Club. Founded in 1886, the Cottage Club (sometimes known as the University Cottage Club) is the second-oldest eating club at Princeton and one of the most traditional. Members are chosen through a selective interview process complete with secret deliberations. The building was designed by a world-renowned architect and set up to mimic an Italian villa with paneling modeled after a palace of Henry VIII. Yearly photos of the club look a bit like an ad for J.Crew or Vineyard

Vines, replete with men in khaki shorts and loafers and women in pastels and sandals.

The second club we picked was Terrace. Known for being liberal and quirky, Terrace was the first club to abandon the restrictive admission process, instead picking members based on a simple lottery system. Meals include vegetarian or vegan options and the club motto is "Food = Love." The club looks more like an Austrian ski haus than a dining hall and has been nicknamed "Mother Terrace" and "the Womb." Members are more hipster than preppy with Chuck Taylors, skirts over tights, and a generally alternative or vintage vibe.

One late afternoon in May, we set up tables in front of each eating club, and offered students $5 for completing a short study. In addition to filling out a quick survey, we took a head-to-toe picture of each student to get a sense of what they were wearing.

Then, we blurred out everything in the photos besides the person's clothes. We concealed the person's face, background, and any other identifying information. It was impossible to tell who someone was and even best friends would have trouble identifying each other from what was left of the photos. All you could see was an outfit.

A few days later, we followed up with people who completed the initial survey. We showed them photos of the other people, one at a time, and asked them a simple question: Which club does this person belong to, Cottage or Terrace?

There are many reasons this question should be hard to answer. After all, the two groups are not *that* different. Both are made up of people who attend the same university, are of the same age, and come from similar socioeconomic backgrounds. It's not like one group was made up of senior citizens and the other of punks dressed in head-to-toe leather.

And members could wear whatever they wanted. There was no required uniform at either club, and students wore a wide range of colors, brands, and styles.

Yet, even though they were given only a tiny bit of information, what top, bottom, and footwear each person happened to be wearing when we snapped the photo, observers had no trouble guessing which club people belonged to. Eighty-five percent of the time they sorted photos into the correct bucket. Cottage Club members were correctly identified as Cottage Club members and Terrace members were correctly identified as Terrace members.

Observers correctly guessed membership because people tended to do the same thing as those around them. Cottage Club members tended to dress like other Cottage Club members and Terrace members tended to dress like other Terrace members.

But that wasn't all. Just like the horizontally striped twosome I observed on my walk, members of a given club dressed similarly, but they didn't dress identically. Cottage Club members tended to dress preppy, but some wore lighter khakis, while others wore darker khakis. Terrace members tended to dress more alternatively, but some wore ripped blue jeans while others wore ripped black jeans. Imitation was at work, but so was differentiation.

And the differentiation wasn't random. Students who reported caring more about being different stood out more. They wore a T-shirt with an unusual dragon pattern or had a bit of lace fringe on the bottom of their preppy skirt.

Students with higher needs for uniqueness still looked enough like their peers that others could guess which club they belonged to, but also dressed in ways that differentiated them from the pack. Similar but different. Consistent but unique.

————————

One might wonder, though, whether clothing choices were really driven by social influence. After all, maybe students with similar tastes joined the same club to be around others like them. Preppy kids might like hanging out with other preppy kids, so they all joined Cottage because it had a reputation as a preppy eating club. Thus, it wasn't that being around other preppy students caused them to dress preppier, they were preppy to begin with, and merely chose to hang out in a place with other preppy folks.*

Alternatively, maybe there were norms that encouraged everyone to dress similarly. Show up to a black-tie formal and no one would be surprised that everyone is wearing similar clothes. It's not about social influence; it's about the norms or rules of the situation.

Most situations don't have such strong norms about how

————————

* This distinction comes up anytime two people are observed acting similarly. Is their similarity due to social influence (i.e., people changed their behavior based on what others were doing), or was it similarity that led the people to interact in the first place. The latter can often be described as homophily, or the tendency of people to interact and become friends with similar others. A great deal of research has shown that people are more likely to associate with similar others. This makes the cause of correlated behavior hard to identify. If two friends both like death metal, is it because of social influence (one liked it, which led the other to like it) or was their shared liking of death metal one of the reasons they became friends in the first place? One benefit of well-designed experiments is that they allow these two explanations to be teased apart.

to behave, but many have implicit guides or suggestions about what to do. Going to the beach? Most people would wear bright, happy colors as opposed to dreary ones. Going out to a nice place for dinner? Might want to dress up a bit. Similarly, groups of guys or girls might all dress similarly on a Friday night because they're going to a type of place where people tend to dress a certain way.

To tease these explanations apart, we conducted a more controlled experiment. I walked around a different college campus and asked people to complete a brief survey. Respondents were shown four options and asked which they would prefer.

The first choice involved cars. Participants choose between a grey Mercedes Sports Sedan, a blue Mercedes Sports Sedan, a grey BMW Coupe, and a blue BMW Coupe.

Another choice involved backpacks, with two different options from each of two brands. Participants were given some information about each product, like how much it cost and some of the features, and then asked to circle whichever option they would buy.

To examine how social influence shaped choice, we also manipulated whether people were given information about what "other people" had chosen.

Half the people made their choices based on just the product information. They were shown the options in each category and made their choice independently.

Other people saw "someone else's" choice before they made their own (similar to the study on line lengths). They were told that, given limited budgets for academic research, each paper survey was designed to be used by multiple people. Rather than just one person completing each survey, two could fill it out, which would save the costs of paper and copying.[18]

Under the question "Which would you buy?" there was a line for two different responses, one labeled "Respondent 1" and one labeled "Respondent 2." If participants did not see any prior answers, they were told to fill in the line labeled "Respondent 1." If the answers of Respondent 1 were marked already, they were asked to fill in the line labeled "Respondent 2."

In actuality, the surveys were rigged. For participants in this social influence condition, we filled in "Respondent 1" to make it look like someone else had picked particular options. In the car category, for example, some participants received a survey that suggested that Respondent 1 picked the grey Mercedes, while others received a survey suggesting Respondent 1 had picked the blue BMW. Thus, each participant was exposed to what they thought was someone else's choice before making their own.

Then, we examined whether students picked the same option as Respondent 1 supposedly chose or something distinct.

Since we randomly picked what Respondent 1 chose, people were not more likely to end up with someone else who naturally had the same preferences as they did.

And unlike a black-tie dinner, or picking what to wear to the beach, there were no norms in either the independent or the social influence condition that should sway how people behaved. We could tease out just how others' choices affected people's behavior.

Imitation would suggest that people just pick whatever the other person selected. Thinking someone chose the grey Mercedes should lead people to choose the same thing.

And differentiation would suggest that people just avoid whatever someone else chose. Knowing someone else picked the grey Mercedes should lead people to avoid that car and spread their choices among the other three options: the blue Mercedes, the grey BMW, or the blue BMW.

But the results were more complex than simply imitation or differentiation alone. Rather than just doing the same thing, or just doing anything different, people chose in ways that allowed them to be similar and different at the same time.

If the other person seemed to select the grey Mercedes, participants tended to choose the blue Mercedes. And if the other person seemed to select the blue BMW, participants tended to choose the grey one. Same brand, just a different color. Similar, but different.

Moderately similar things blend the old and the new. The novel and the familiar. But they also satisfy our need to be optimally distinct.

As the study of line lengths or the story of J. K. Rowling demonstrate, humans strive for validation. We want to be part of something. Being similar to, or doing the same thing as, others gives us confidence that we are doing something right.

But just like siblings who want to distinguish themselves from an older brother or sister, we also have a drive for differentiation. We don't want to be the same as everyone else, we want to be different, unique. We like things that allow us to separate ourselves from the crowd.

These two motives seem opposing. We want to be similar but we want to be different. We want to do the same thing as others but we also want to be special.

Moderate similarity helps resolve this tension. We wear the same brands as our friends, but we pick out different styles. We buy the same couch as our coworker, but pick a different color.

By choosing similarly to those around us, or groups we want to be a part of, we satisfy our need to fit in. But by not choosing the exact same thing, we satisfy our need to be different.

We are distinct, but optimally so.

Even the attributes people choose to differentiate themselves on are shaped by optimal distinctiveness. As the story of Snooki and the free Gucci bag or the geeks and the wristbands illustrate, brands and other aspects of choice often signal particular identities. If someone wears Nike clothes all the time, other people might assume that person is athletic, while if someone wears Gucci, people might infer that she cares about fashion.

In these situations, brand is an *identity-relevant attribute*. It communicates information about the social identity and preferences of the person wearing the brand.

Other attributes, however, may not be as identity relevant. Whether someone is wearing a blue or black shirt, for example, doesn't tell observers much about her. Similarly, in most situations, wearing a tank top versus a T-shirt doesn't provide much of a signal.

Consequently, people that want to signal particular identities while also feeling unique often conform on identity-relevant attributes while differentiating themselves on identity-irrelevant ones. Newly minted lawyers often buy BMWs to show that they've made it; so a lawyer that wants to signal while standing out will buy an orange one. Picking the brand that communicates the desired information but an unusual color separates them from the pack. If Fendi is making the "it" handbag this season, fashionistas may all buy Fendis, but try to pick colors that are less popular.*

---

* In other situations, color may be identity relevant, while other dimensions

What will be popular next year? No one can say for sure. That said, it's also not as random as one might think. Things that have features in common with what's been popular recently have a leg up on the competition. Similar enough to evoke the warm glow of familiarity, but different enough to feel novel and fresh.

So when trying to predict the Color of the Year, or fill in the popular expression "_____ is the new black," the answer might just be slate grey.

PUTTING SOCIAL INFLUENCE TO WORK

Integrating similarity and difference is particularly important when managing innovation. How should a new product like the Swiffer be described? Is it a revolutionary mop? A new cleaning tool? And how should it be designed? Should seats in driverless cars face forward because that is what people are used to, even if that is no longer required?

A new product or technology can be light-years ahead of the competition, but its success hinges on consumer perception. If the product seems too similar to what's already out there, people aren't compelled to purchase. If this year's iWidget seems just like last year's, why pay the extra money to replace the old one? If the innovation is too radical, though, other issues arise. Consumers don't know how to categorize it (what is a Swiffer, anyway?), they don't understand what it does, and they can't tell if they

---

provide differentiation. Goths and punks often wear all black, but one goth might wear a black trench coat while another wears a black T-shirt. Similarly, if the color peach is in vogue, people who want to seem fashionable may all wear peach but buy the color from different brands. The particular attributes that people conform and differentiate on will depend on which attributes communicate identity and which ones don't.

really need it. Both extremes are dangerous, and carefully navigating the sweet spot in between requires effectively blending similarity and difference.

Take the introduction of the automobile. Horses had been the primary mode of transportation, but they were restrictive. Travel was slow, expensive, and even dangerous. Horse-drawn vehicles had an engine with a mind of its own, and the fatality rate in cities like Chicago were seven times what they are for cars today.

Automobiles promised a solution. They could go farther, faster, and even cut down on manure, which at the time was threatening to overrun major cities.

But getting people to adopt these early cars required a huge mind shift. Horses (and donkeys) had been the primary transportation method for thousands of years. While there were many drawbacks to this method, people were comfortable with it. They knew what to expect.

Automobiles were completely new. They required different fuel to run, different skills to drive, and different know-how to fix.

These changes required some getting used to. The first time people saw a carriage roll down the street without a horse in front, they were shocked. Rural Americans viewed this "Devil's Wagon" as symbolizing the decadence of the city, and introduced restrictive laws to block its intrusion.[19] Horses, skittish to begin with, were spooked by these loud, rambling horseless carriages and prone to run away, taking their passengers careening with them.

In 1899, a clever inventor proposed a solution to make people, and horses, more comfortable. Named the Horsey Horseless, it involved taking a life-size replica of a horse head, down to the shoulders, and attaching it to the front of a carriage.

The buggy had the appearance of a horse-drawn vehicle, and thus horses, and their human riders, would be less likely to be scared when it passed by. The fake head also could be used as a gas tank.

It's easy to laugh at a fake horse head glued to the front of a car. It seems silly, almost comical. But while it might seem ridiculous today, it's hard to imagine how scary cars were when they were first introduced. Why not add something recognizable on the front to make the novelty less threatening?

More generally, successfully introducing radical innovations often involves cloaking technology in a skin of familiarity.[20] When TiVo introduced what we think of today as a digital video recorder, they had a similar challenge to the automobile. The technology was innovative and had the potential to create a completely new market. But success required getting consumers to shift their behavior. From passively watching television to actively directing what they wanted to watch and when.

So, to help the transition, and make it easier for consumers to understand the service, TiVo designed their device to look like a VCR. A black, rectangular device that sat below the TV or above the cable box, just like a regular VCR or DVD player would.

Pry open a DVR and a VCR (if you can find one), though, and the guts are completely different. A VCR is like an old film camera. Film, in this case long plastic tape, winds through the device and content gets recorded on it (or played from it).

TiVo is nothing like that. As the name implies, digital video recorders are actually a computer. There's no film that needs to wind through anything.

As a result, there was no need for the device to look anything like a VCR. It could have been shaped like a standard desktop computer, colored bright blue, or made into a pyramid.

But by using a familiar form, TiVo made people more comfortable adopting this radical innovation. By hiding the technology in something that looked visually familiar, TiVo used similarity to make difference feel more palatable.*

Many digital actions today visually evoke their analog ancestors. We click on the icon of a floppy disk to save documents and drag digital files to be thrown away in what looks like a waste bin. Visual similarity also shows up offline. High-end cars use fake wood grain on the dashboard and veggie burgers often have grill marks. All make the different seem more similar.[21]

---

* Such visual cues not only make novel technology feel more familiar, they also shape the reference category used to evaluate the device. Apple's Newton was an early predecessor to today's smartphone. It was designed and viewed as a computer, and ultimately evaluated as an underperforming one. The PalmPilot was introduced only a few years later, but because it fit in a pocket and resembled a daily agenda book, that, instead of a computer, became the standard of comparison. And seen as an improvement over the standard agenda book, the PalmPilot became quite successful.

The opposite also holds. Design can be used to make incremental innovations feel more novel. When Apple introduced the iMac in 1998, it featured only minor technological improvements. But from a visual standpoint it was radically different. Rather than the same old black or grey box, the iMac was shaped like a gum drop and came in colors like tangerine and strawberry. The device was hugely successful, and design, rather than technology, created the needed sense of difference that encouraged people to purchase.

Technology is never evaluated alone. Design and technology combine to shape consumer perceptions, and the combination is more effective when it makes innovations seem optimally distinct.

Even without us realizing it, other people are constantly influencing what we think, buy, and do. But does social influence go even further? Could it influence how hard we're driven to achieve? Whether we're motivated to work harder or give up and quit?

5. Come On Baby, Light My Fire

Kara sat quietly in the dark waiting for the race to begin. It would be a sprint. Nothing complicated, just a straight track. No curves to stumble around, no turns to navigate. Just one long stretch lay out in front of her. It was a distance she had run many times.

Sometimes she ran against others, but today she was running alone. Just her and the clock, slowly ticking off the seconds that made up her time.

She could hear the steady pounding of the fans in the grandstands. Her peers milling around, ready for the start. They had already seen five racers go by, and Kara would be the sixth. All this buildup for less than a minute of action.

When the light went off, Kara jumped out of the gate. She started slow but picked up speed. Sprinting down the track, trying to focus on the end and ignore the eyes fixed on her. She felt scared, frightened even, but she kept churning, one foot in front of the other. Finally, after a tense forty-two seconds, she reached the finish line, gasping for air. It was her best time so far.

As the black door shut behind her, Kara retreated to a corner. She stretched each of her six legs and groomed her antennae.

Kara was a cockroach.

In the late 1800s researcher Norman Triplett published a study that marked the birth of a field we now know as social psychology.[1] For his master's thesis at Indiana University, Triplett examined race data from over two thousand cyclists. Cyclists raced one of three ways. Sometimes they raced alone, simply trying to score the best time. Sometimes they raced head-to-head in direct competition with other cyclists. And sometimes they raced against the clock, but with another cyclist racing with them to set the pace.

When he compared the times turned in by different racers, Triplett noticed that cyclists raced faster when they biked at the same time. Whether competing or not, people who biked with others cycled twenty to thirty seconds faster per mile. Racing together seemed to improve performance.[2]

To probe this idea further, Triplett designed an experiment. He took a group of children and had them play a game that involved turning a fishing reel as quickly as possible. A flag was attached to the fishing line, and Triplett timed how quickly it took the kids to wind the reel, either working alone, or working side by side with another child who was playing the same game.

The results were similar to what he'd observed among cyclists: kids reeled faster when another child was reeling next to them.

Many subsequent studies have found the same pattern. The mere presence of others changes performance. People tend to do better when others are around.

In one experiment,[3] college students were shown a word and given a minute to write down as many related words as they could think of. In another, students were given a passage to read and asked to write as many arguments as possible disproving the line of thinking in the reading. In both cases, people who did the tasks in groups (working individually, but in the presence of others) performed better. They generated more word associations and more arguments against the passage.

This phenomenon has been described as social facilitation, where the presence of others leads people to perform faster and better than they would otherwise. Even if people aren't collaborating, or competing, the mere fact that others are present changes behavior.

And it's not just people that show social facilitation. Animals behave the same way.[4] Rats drink faster and explore more when other rats are around. Monkeys work harder on a simple task when other monkeys are present, and dogs run faster in pairs than alone. Ants dig three times as much sand when working alongside other ants, even if they aren't cooperating. Social facilitation even impacts how much animals eat. The presence of a peer eating leads chickens to keep eating, even if they are already full.

Across a host of situations, people (and animals) seem to perform better when others are present.*

---

* Research on social facilitation can be classified into two main areas: research that examines audience effects and research that examines coaction effects. The former examines how the presence of passive spectators influences performance. How running alone, versus with others watching, affects how quickly people run. The latter examines how others doing the *same* activity separately, but at the same time, influences performance. How running alone, versus next to someone else who is running, affects how quickly people run. In both cases, the presence of others can influence performance, and for similar reasons.

Interestingly though, other studies have found the opposite. That people do *worse* when others are present.[5]

In one study, college students were given the difficult task of remembering a list of nonsense syllables. Those who learned the list in front of an audience took longer to learn and made more errors. In another, people were asked to trace a maze while blindfolded. Participants took longer when spectators were present. And people taking their driving test were less likely to pass if others, besides the instructor, were present in the car.

The presence of others has also been found to decrease performance in animals.[6] When paired together, greenfinches had more difficulty discriminating between palatable and unpalatable food sources. Parakeets took longer to learn a maze, and made more errors, when trained in pairs.

So which is it? Does having others around facilitate performance or inhibit it?

This question vexed Stanford professor Bob Zajonc. Zajonc's path to academia was far from usual.[7] An only child born in Poland in the 1920s, Zajonc's family fled to Warsaw in 1939 to avoid the Nazis. Two weeks after they arrived, however, the relative's apartment they were staying in was hit in an air raid, and Zajonc's parents were killed.

Zajonc barely survived with broken legs, and the sixteen-year-old's hospital stay was cut short when the Nazis arrested him and sent him to a German labor camp. Zajonc managed to escape with two other prisoners by walking over 200 miles into France. After crossing the border, the Germans captured them and sent them to a French jail. Eventually, Zajonc escaped again, staging a breakout and joining the French Resistance. He and a fellow prisoner walked for almost 550 miles, stealing food and clothes along the way, before a generous fisherman found them and brought them to Ireland.

From there, Zajonc made his way to England. Having learned English, French, and German through his journeys, he became a translator for the U.S. Army. When the war ended, he worked briefly for the United Nations before emigrating to the United States. Zajonc applied to be an undergraduate at the University of Michigan and was eventually accepted on a probationary basis. He worked through a bachelor's and a master's, and in 1955 he received his PhD from Michigan in social psychology.

As a scientist, Zajonc had a knack for dusting off important questions that had been overlooked for decades and cleverly reinventing them with strokes of insight. He had a keen sense of human behavior and was always looking for simple relationships underlying complex patterns. It was with this perspective that he studied social facilitation.

The findings seemed to contradict each other. On the one hand, numerous studies had shown that the mere presence of others improved performance. That an audience, or others doing the same task, made people perform faster or do more, even in the absence of competition. On the other hand, a similarly compelling set of results showed the opposite. That the presence of others could impair learning and performance.

Zajonc had a theory about what explained the differing outcomes. It was as elegant as it was simple.

He just needed a way to test it. And that's where Kara came in.

Picture in your mind an Olympic 400-meter track race. A large, burgundy-red track surrounded by stands. A stadium, filled to the brim with screaming fans, each cheering on their countrymen to victory. And competitors, lined up, awaiting the starting gun.

Now imagine that same picture, but replace all the people with . . . cockroaches. Instead of muscular sprinters cloaked in spandex, the competitors are . . . cockroaches. And instead of camera-toting, flag-waving, vuvuzela-blaring supporters, the fans are . . . well, cockroaches.

Ugh.

People tend to react to cockroaches with disgust. Scuttling pests that feed on rotting food and thrive in the darkness.

But cockroaches are actually some of the cleanest and hardiest insects. They can survive without air for forty-five minutes and recover from being submerged in water for a half hour. They can endure decapitation, at least temporarily, and a cockroach's severed head can subsist for several hours, or even longer when refrigerated and given food (though it's not clear why anyone would want to do that.)

Zajonc thought cockroaches would be the perfect subjects to test social facilitation.

So he built a cockroach stadium. A large Plexiglas cube where he could time how quickly cockroaches ran through a set course. On one side of the cube was a small, dark starting box where the cockroach waited for the race to start, separated from the track by a thin metal door. On another side of the cube was the finish line, another small, dark box separated from the track by a similar metal door.

Cockroaches hate light. So, rather than using a starting gun to drive them to action, Zajonc used a floodlight. He would open the doors covering the entrance and exit to the track and flick on a bright light in the starting box. The cockroach would scuttle onto the track, looking for a dark place to hide. Light filled the entire track, so the only escape was the finishing box. When the roach finally scampered in, Zajonc would shut the door and return the roach to darkness.

Zajonc timed how long it took the roach to run from one box to another. From when he opened the door on one end to when he closed it on the other.

To test how the presence of others influenced performance, Zajonc also built cockroach stands. Little audience boxes filled with other cockroaches situated next to the track. To make it easy to see the fans, but keep them out of the action, a clear wall separated them from the racetrack. By removing the audience boxes for some of the races, and keeping them in for others, Zajonc could test whether the mere presence of others, other cockroaches in this case, changed how quickly the racers ran.

All this was extremely clever. Genius, even. But there was one more key detail.

Zajonc thought he knew why others' presence was having opposing effects. Why others sometimes increased performance and sometimes decreased it.

In his mind, it depended on the complexity of the task, or the thing on which people (or animals) were being measured. If the task was easy, or something participants had done many times before, spectators would facilitate performance. But if the task was difficult, or involved learning something new, spectators would inhibit performance.

To test this idea, he created two versions of the track. One was a straightaway. The starting box on one end and the finishing box on the other. Nothing could be simpler. The cockroach only had one way to run and its dominant response should be to run away from the light and toward the end.

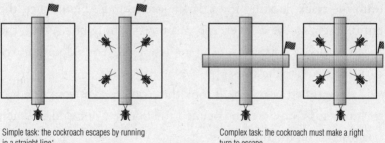

Simple task: the cockroach escapes by running in a straight line.   Complex task: the cockroach must make a right turn to escape.

The other track was much more complex. Halfway down the straight track, a second track ran perpendicular to the first like a cross. Rather than only one way to run, the cockroach now had three. But only one led to safety.

And rather than being placed in the easiest spot, at the opposite end of the starting box, the finishing box was placed on one of the sides. So the roach had to run straight, make a right or left turn, and run some more before reaching the end. It couldn't just run blindly, it had to try different options to learn which one was correct.

Not surprisingly, it took the roaches longer to run the more complex track. They had to figure out which way to go and needed three times as long to finish.

But the audience also influenced performance. On the straightaway, roaches ran faster when the audience was present, chopping almost a third off their time. But for the more complex track, others had the opposite impact. An audience led the roaches to run slower, increasing their time by almost a third.

Zajonc was right. Whether others help or hurt performance depends on the complexity of the task.[8]

In the decades following this seminal study, the same pattern has been found again and again. Having others around improves performance (e.g., speed and accuracy) on easy, well-learned tasks, but decreases performance on unfamiliar, and thus more difficult, tasks.

Others make us faster at tying our own shoes, for example, but slower at tying a bow tie (at least for most of us who don't tie one often).[9] Skilled pool players make more shots when others are watching, but unskilled players miss more.[10] Having an audience makes us faster at taking notes, unless we're taking notes with our non-dominant hand. If we're right-handed, having someone else watching makes writing with our left hand slower.

If you've ever gone to the gym with a friend, or run next to someone on the treadmill, you've probably experienced the positive impact of others. Even though you're not competing, their presence helps. You lift a little harder or run a little faster.

But if you've ever had someone watch you while you parallel park, you've also probably felt others' negative impact. Parallel parking is never easy, but other people often make it more difficult. You thought you were pulling in just fine, but it ends up you turned too late, so you have to pull out and start over. Other cars start pulling up behind you on the street. You take another pass, but this time you cut it too tight, so you have to start again. By now your passenger starts looking at you like you need to go back to driving school.

Some of us are just bad at parking, but social facilitation is also playing a role. Having someone watch makes the (somewhat) difficult task of parallel parking take longer.

Whether helping or hurting performance, social facilitation happens for a few reasons.[11] First, others can be distracting. They take attention away from parallel parking or whatever else we are trying to do. Second, others increase impression management.

We want to look good to others, so we try harder. Third, in part due to impression management, others increase physiological arousal. Our heart rate quickens, our blood pumps faster, and our body readies for action.

These factors lead us to do better at things that are automatic, natural, or well learned. We feel challenged, our competitive juices start flowing, and we spring to action. Faced with something we're pretty good at (e.g., running on a treadmill or doing an exercise we've done a hundred times before), we perform even better.

But for tasks that are more difficult or require more attention, those same factors make us do worse. *What are they thinking? Are they going to judge me if I park badly?* We feel threatened and anxious. We're worried about failing or doing badly. And that leads us to perform worse.[12]

ENERGY BILL 2.0

Have you checked your e-mail today?

For many people, that's not even a question. Most would say yes. Of course. You've probably checked your e-mail in the last hour. You might have even checked it while reading this chapter.

And what about the weather? Have you checked that today? This week? How about sports scores or social media?

While we may not check these things as frequently as our e-mail, we certainly check them a lot. We have a decent sense of what the weather will be like this week, how our local team is doing, and how pretty it was in Aruba when our high school classmate went there on vacation (thank goodness for social media).

But what about your household energy use? How much

power you or your family are using in your home or apartment. Have you checked that today? This week? Ever?

Energy use is one of the biggest challenges facing society. But while everyone realizes it's important, solving the problem may be less about technology and more about social influence.

Climate change is one of the most pressing global concerns of the twenty-first century. Regardless of your political bent, it's tough not to at least acknowledge the overwhelming scientific evidence that temperatures are rising. Glaciers are retreating and subtropical deserts are expanding. Extreme weather events such as droughts and heavy snowfalls are more frequent, species of plants and animals are vanishing, and food security is threatened as crop yields decrease.

Energy use lies at the core of these global warming trends. Burning fossil fuels generates carbon dioxide, and greenhouse gases emitted from cars, factories, and power plants continue to rise. As the world economy grows, people are using more and more energy. It takes energy to keep us warm in the winter and cool in the summer. It takes energy to power our computers and run our factories. And it takes energy to get us to work and back home again. As more of the world industrializes, a greater and greater strain is put on our natural resources.

Something has to give. Either we figure out a way to cut down and clean up energy use, or the world is on a course for some unsettling changes.

Many of the proposed solutions are sizable in scale. Government regulations such as capping the amount of carbon dioxide power plants can produce or standards that require automakers to achieve a certain number of miles per gallon. Other solutions focus on new technologies and alternative energy. Solar and wind farms have become more prevalent, and exciting developments in geothermal energy have enabled us to harness the warmth of the earth's core.

Attempts to shift consumer behavior also focus on big changes. Buy an Energy Star washer that saves water and uses less energy per load. Swap out your old lightbulbs for compact fluorescents that may last up to ten times longer. Even your attic can be improved through more effective insulation.

One of the simplest solutions, though, is just getting people to conserve energy. Flip the lights off when you leave the room and take shorter showers. Turn the heat down a degree or two in the winter and leave it on low when you leave the house. When added up across the population, small changes in energy conservation can have a big impact.

So how do we get people to change their behavior?

If you had to pick someone who would revolutionize the power industry, Dan Yates would have been an unlikely choice. An expert pole vaulter from San Diego, Yates came to Harvard with almost shoulder-length hair. He graduated a few years later with a degree in computer science and an interest in entrepreneurship.

Yates moved to San Francisco, and after a short stint with one company, he cofounded an educational assessment software business with a classmate from Harvard. The company did well, and after three years had over 140 employees and close to 500 school districts as customers. Publishing powerhouse Houghton Mifflin became interested, and Yates and his cofounder sold the business.

After working at Houghton for a year, Yates needed a break. So he and his wife planned a yearlong adventure they would never forget. They bought a used Toyota 4Runner, started in Alaska, and traversed the entire length of the Pan-American Highway. Around 30,000 miles down to Ushuaia, on the southernmost tip of Argentina.

It was a beautiful journey. They saw rare animals in southwest Bolivia and majestic tree canopies in the cloud forest of Costa Rica.

But Yates and his wife also witnessed lots of environmental devastation. Acres of rain forest that had been leveled. Patches of brush and nature that had been set ablaze to clear the area for farming. Yates came back from the trip wondering what he could do to help the environment.

With another classmate from Harvard, Alex Laskey, Yates started thinking about ways to reduce energy waste. He and his partner bandied around a bunch of ideas. Some around solar power and some around reducing emissions.

But the most promising direction came when Yates looked at his electricity bill. It was a mess. Systems delivery charges, power adjustments, and regulatory fees, not to mention confusing terms such as kilowatt hours and therms. There were dozens of fields to pay attention to, and the information was hard, if not impossible, to parse. Yates thought there could be something better. "I didn't understand what kilowatt hours were; I didn't know what therms were. I didn't care to know. I just wanted to know how much energy I used compared to my neighbor or something else I could understand."[13]

Yates wasn't alone. Most people find their energy bills so confusing that they don't even try to understand the details. They just pay the bill every month and move on.

Maybe social influence could help.

San Marcos is a great place to study energy conservation.[14] Thirty-five miles north of San Diego, the city is tucked just inland off where Interstate 5 hugs the coast. Southern California is known for its sunshine, and San Marcos doesn't disappoint. The city gets less than half the amount of rain as the rest of the United States and is sunny more than 260 days a year.

In the winter, though, San Marcos can get cold enough that people need to turn on the heat. And when summer swelters, residents blast air-conditioning. The broader area is also plagued by drought, and every few years restrictions kick in around water use. People can only wash their cars certain times of day, and residents can only water their lawn certain days of the week, depending on where they live. Citizens aren't thinking about energy use all the time, but it's lurking in the background.

One dry summer day, over a decade ago, Professors Bob Cialdini, Wes Schultz, Jessica Nolan, Noah Goldstein, and Vladas Griskevicius ran a simple experiment in San Marcos.

Graduate students went door-to-door in the community, delivering persuasive messages promoting energy conservation. Each household received a door hanger (similar to the DO NOT DISTURB sign at a hotel) encouraging people to use less energy. The door hanger promoted using fans, taking shorter showers, and turning off the air-conditioning at night.

When trying to change behavior, energy conservation campaigns usually focus on one of three overarching appeals: saving money, helping the environment, or promoting social responsibility. To test which type of appeal was more effective, homes were divided into groups, and each group received different messaging.

Some homeowners received an appeal that highlighted saving money. When talking about fans, for example, the appeal stated, "Summer is here and the time is right for saving money on your home energy bill. How can you save money this summer? By using fans instead of air conditioning! Why? According to researchers at Cal State San Marcos, you could save up to $54 per month by using fans instead of air conditioning to keep cool in the summer."

A second group got an environmental message. It encouraged people to "Protect the Environment by Conserving Energy. Summer is here and the time is right for reducing greenhouse gases. How can you protect the environment this summer? By using fans instead of air conditioning! Why? According to researchers at Cal State San Marcos, you can prevent the release of up to 262 pounds of greenhouse gases per month by using fans instead of air conditioning to keep cool this summer! Using fans instead of air conditioning—The Environmental Choice."

A third group received a message about being good citizens: "Summer is here and we need to work together to conserve energy. How can you conserve energy for future generations? By using fans instead of air conditioning! Why? According to researchers at Cal State San Marcos, you can reduce your monthly demand for electricity by 29% by using fans instead of air conditioning to keep cool this summer! Using fans instead of air conditioning—The Socially Responsible Choice."

In addition to passing out different appeals, the researchers also measured how much energy different households used, both before and after they received the conservation messages.

Most people guessed that the environmental appeal would work best. Not leaps and bounds better than talking about saving money or helping the community, but at least somewhat more effective.

But they were wrong. None of the appeals worked. The conservation messages had zero impact on energy consumption. Whether the appeals encouraged people to help the environment, save money, or just be a good citizen, people didn't budge. They didn't use any less energy than they had before. It was almost as if the messages had never been delivered at all.

Fortunately, the researchers also tried a fourth appeal. Rather than seeking to convince people to conserve energy by pointing out different reasons for doing so, this appeal simply highlighted social norms; what other people in the community were doing. "When surveyed, 77% of your neighbors use fans instead of air-conditioning to keep cool in the summer. Turn off your air conditioning and turn on your fans."

And people did. Households that received this message decreased their energy use significantly. And this reduced consumption persisted even weeks after they received the last appeal. Simply telling people that their neighbors were saving energy led them to conserve more themselves.

Building on these findings, Yates and Laskey saw an opportunity. Social norms could provide a simple and cost-effective way to reduce people's energy use. Coupling usage data with information about what others were doing could make for a more effective energy bill.

Their company, Opower, now works with more than one hundred utility companies worldwide. Opower sends consumers carefully targeted energy reports. Rather than confusing terminology, the reports help consumers understand how much energy they are using by putting their usage in context. Designed based on the San Marcos study findings, the energy reports show consumers their consumption relative to similar households nearby. Whether they are using more or less energy than their peers.

Social comparison information motivates consumers, but the reports don't stop there. They pair that information with specific customized steps different consumers can take to save energy: replacing certain electronics, turning off lights, and adjusting the settings on the television.

These programs lead people to reduce their energy consumption by around 2 percent.[15] For a given person, this decrease may not seem huge, but aggregated across the country the impact is staggering. Since their launch, Opower's programs have helped save more than 6 terawatt-hours of energy.[16] That's 6 trillion watt-hours, or the equivalent to taking all the homes in Alaska and Hawaii, more than 2.1 million people, off the power grid for an entire year.

Opower hasn't just saved energy though; it has also helped reduce carbon dioxide emissions. The cumulative impact of these reduced emissions is equal to saving more than twenty-four thousand football fields' worth of American forests or taking almost all the cars in Chicago off the road for a year.

Not bad for a little feedback about performance relative to others.

Interestingly, when asked in advance about whether this appeal would work, most San Marcos residents thought it would fail. Did they care about whether their friends and neighbors were conserving energy? A little, but they said that wasn't as important to them as helping the environment or saving money.

But they were wrong. As people often do, they underestimated how big an impact others have on behavior.

It's clear that others can motivate us to work harder or save energy, but does it matter how our performance stacks up to theirs?

THE UPSIDE OF LOSING

You may not be into sports betting, but imagine for a moment that someone gave you $10,000 to bet on a basketball game. At halftime, you choose whichever team you think will win. If you win, you get to keep the money, and if you lose, well, you end up with nothing.

After pinching yourself at your good fortune (and your friend's generosity), you focus on picking which team to bet on. It's a fast-paced game and both teams show promise. The lead changes back and forth until one team goes on a run to lead by eight points. The other team charges back, closing the gap and resulting in another string of lead changes. At the end of the first half, one team (call them the Washington Winners) is ahead of the other team (call them the Louisville Losers) by a point.

Which team would you bet your $10,000 on to win? The team that is winning or the team that is losing?

If you're like most people, you probably picked the team that was winning. After all, whether fighting to win a tough game or trying to be the top salesperson in your office, intuition suggests that being ahead increases the chance of winning. Hockey teams leading after the first period win over two-thirds of their games, and baseball teams leading after three innings win over three fourths of the time. Basketball is no different. Teams that are winning tend to win and this tendency gets stronger as the lead gets larger. Teams ahead by four at halftime, for example, win about 60 percent of games. Teams up by eight win over 80 percent of the time.

This tendency should come as no surprise. Teams that are winning tend to be better teams. That's partially why they're ahead.

Losing teams also have further to go to win. Mechanically, they have to score that many more points than their opponents if they hope to pull out a victory.

But could being behind sometimes be a good thing? Could losing sometimes actually make people more likely to win?

One of the most enjoyable, yet challenging things I've ever done was coach youth soccer. I was looking for a fun extracurricular activity in college, something that would take my mind off school, when a friend mentioned a Nike program that encouraged college kids to teach youth sports. My dad had coached when I was young, and I had always loved soccer, so I thought I'd give it a shot.

For the next few months, I spent every Tuesday and Thursday afternoon with eighteen boys from the East Palo Alto division of the American Youth Soccer Organization. I was part teacher, part chaperone for a group of wonderful but crazy eleven- and twelve-year-old boys. We ran laps to improve conditioning, did passing drills to develop teamwork, and dribbled around cones to build confidence and competence. We also did a lot of goofing off and chasing each other around the field. I wasn't the best coach, but I tried to impart what little knowledge I had about the game and help them become better players.

In general, we were a strong team. We had a tall, smart-aleck forward with a deft touch and another shorter speedster who scored a lot of goals. We had a couple of strong defenders and some crafty midfielders who never seemed to tire of running up and down the field.

But when it came to games, we were a mixed bag. Sometimes we played great. The first time the kids executed a "give-and-go," I almost cried. It was amazing to see them internalize what we had learned in practice.

Other times we just fell apart. Something we had drilled dozens of times week after week just didn't seem to stick. No matter how many times we practiced, we could never make it work.

As a coach, there was little to do but pace the sidelines. It's one thing to have a plan about how to get better at something, but it's another to try to motivate others. I could substitute here and there, but the kids controlled the game.

The one chance I had to shake it up was at halftime. We'd form a halfhearted circle in the grass, the kids would guzzle water and eat orange slices, and we'd talk tactics. What we were doing well and what we needed to improve. Here and there I tried to throw in a bit of inspiration. A little bit of "You can do it!" or "Go out and get 'em!" The kids would then go play the second half, mostly indifferent to whatever I'd tried to highlight during the break.

But while the speech didn't seem to change how we played, whether we were winning or losing did. If we were winning or tied going into the break, we played okay. Sometimes we'd win and sometimes we'd lose. But if we were losing at halftime, something different happened. The kids seemed more motivated. We'd go into the half down 0–1 and come out winning 3–2. Or we'd be down two goals, 1–3, but finish the game winning 5–3. We seemed to play better when we were behind.

As a coach, this drove me nuts. If we could come from behind and win, why couldn't we play that well *all* the time? It was clear we had the skills and the drive, so why did it only seem to come out when we were losing?

———————

There are many reasons any one team might win or lose any one game: team chemistry, skill, home-field advantage, even the weather. But might my team's performance illustrate a larger pattern?

Behavioral economist Devin Pope and I decided to find out. Soccer is a low-scoring sport, and it would be tough to amass enough kids' games to form a meaningful dataset, so we examined professional basketball instead.

We analyzed more than fifteen years of play. Almost twenty thousand NBA games overall. Everything from David Robinson's games with the Spurs to Paul Pierce, Ray Allen, and Kevin Garnett's games with the Celtics. We recorded the score at halftime, as well as which team ended up winning the game.

Consistent with the proverbial home-team advantage, teams were more likely to win when they played at home than on the road. Better teams, as indicated by a higher season winning percentage, were also more likely to win. And, not surprisingly, the further ahead teams were at halftime, the more likely they were to win. For every two points a team was doing better relative to its opponent (e.g., up by two versus tied or up by four instead of two), they were around 7 percent more likely to win the game.

This makes sense. Winning leads to winning.

Except at one place. Right around zero. Right where teams shifted from losing to winning.

Take teams losing by a point. Everything else would suggest these teams should be about 7 percent less likely to win than teams ahead by a point. Controlling for how good each team was, whether they were playing at home or not, and all the other factors, out of one hundred games, teams losing by one point at halftime should have won seven fewer games than teams winning by a point.

But they didn't.

In fact, teams that were losing by a point were actually more likely to win. Not only did being behind increase a team's chance of winning (by around 8 percent), but, compared to their opponents, teams that were behind by one actually won *more* games. Even though they tended to be worse teams and had to score more points than their opponents to win.[17]

If you had to bet money, betting on the team down by one at halftime would be a safer bet.*

Why does losing lead to winning? To find out, we had people play a simple game.

Imagine sitting in front of a computer keyboard. On the left side of the keyboard, right below the letter Q, is the A key. Toward the bottom of the keyboard, right between the letters V and N is the B key. Place one finger on the A key, and one finger on the B key, and imagine pressing them, in short succession, as quickly as possible. A, B, A, B, A, B, as fast as you can.

Every time you press those two keys in order, you get a

---

* The same holds for college basketball. Analyzing more than forty-five thousand games showed that being behind at halftime significantly increased NCAA teams' chance of winning. Slight underdogs are also more likely to win. Since the NCAA tournament expanded to sixty-four teams, ninth seeds have beaten eighth seeds 54 percent of the time. Not a huge margin, but surprising given that the eighth seeds should be the better teams.

point. The faster you mash on those two keys, the more points you get. Not the most fun game in the world, but pretty easy to play.

Now imagine that you are competing against someone else who is playing the same game. There are two thirty-second halves (or periods of play) divided by a short break (or halftime). Whichever player has the most points at the end of the game wins a small sum of money.

We told different groups of players different things during halftime. While some players were told nothing, other players were given competitive feedback. Similar to Opower's energy reports, they were given information about how well they were doing relative to others.

To examine the effect of being behind, we rigged the competitive feedback. We told players that their opponent had scored one point more than they had so far, and thus they were one point behind. Then we measured how hard people worked in the second half of the game. Whether they increased or decreased the number of keys pressed.

Thinking they were behind increased motivation. It made people work harder. Compared to participants that received no feedback at all, those who thought they were behind increased their effort more than threefold.*

---

* This experiment also rules out some of the things we couldn't control for in the basketball data. Maybe referees root for the underdog and give losing teams a break, calling fewer fouls and giving them a better chance to win. Or maybe coaches are better at motivating their players when their team is behind rather than ahead. Other tests we ran cast doubt on those possibilities, but even then, we can't rule them out in that data. But in the experiment we can. Even when there were no coaches, or referees, people worked harder when they thought they were slightly behind their opponent.

Competition influences motivation by shaping people's reference points, or the yardstick they use to measure how well they are doing. When running a 5K race, taking a test, or making sales calls at the office, we often set goals for ourselves. We want to run the race in under twenty minutes, get an A, or bring in ten new clients this month.

Our performance relative to those goals, in turn, affects how hard we continue to work. Consider the following:

> *Chip and George both love to work out and each usually follows a workout plan that involves twenty-five sit-ups a day. One day, Chip sets a goal of performing thirty-seven sit-ups and George sets a goal of performing thirty-three sit-ups. Both Chip and George are tired after performing thirty-five sit-ups and, at most, have the energy to perform one, maybe two more.*

Who do you think will work harder to perform those final couple sit-ups? Chip or George?

People tend to think that Chip will work harder than George to do the last couple sit-ups because he's yet to reach his goal.[18] He has only done thirty-five and his goal was thirty-seven. Chip is almost there and with just a little more effort he can achieve what he set out to do. While George probably feels good because he's achieved his goal, Chip may feel unsatisfied because he hasn't gotten there yet. And that dissatisfaction will motivate him to work harder. Compared to being ahead, being behind is more motivating.[19]

The motivating effect of being behind happens not only for the overall goal, it also happens for progress along the way. If our goal is to bring in ten new clients this month, and halfway through we've only brought in four, we'll feel less satisfied than if we've already brought in eight. Being behind our ideal trajectory can motivate us to work harder.

Competition affects motivation for similar reasons. Just as we use certain predetermined goals (thirty-three sit-ups or ten new clients) to determine whether we are succeeding, we often use others as a standard of comparison. Winning a basketball game doesn't depend just on how many points your team scores; it depends on scoring more than the other team. Is 1,074 kilowatt-hours a lot of energy to use in a month? Hard to say, but if someone's neighbors are using less than that, people may be motivated to close the gap.

Sometimes there is a clear and compelling reward for doing better than others. Whoever makes the most sales calls gets a bonus. Whoever shoots the lowest wins the golf tournament.

Other times, the reward is just the feeling of achievement. Winning is more satisfying than losing. Using less energy than your neighbor feels better than using more.

Consequently, being behind others can motivate us to perform better. Teams losing by one at halftime came out of the locker room fired up. They played hard and erased most of the deficit in the first few minutes of the second half. Just like the people pressing the *A* and *B* keys in our experiment, being behind motivated the players to work harder. And as a result, their teams were more likely to win.

But is being behind always more motivating?

WHEN LOSING LEADS TO . . . LOSING WORSE

Richard "Pancho" Gonzales was one of the best tennis players of all time. Born in Los Angeles, California, in 1928, Gonzales is one of the game's few Mexican-American stars. His mother gave him a fifty-one-cent racquet when he was twelve years old and he never looked back. Largely self-taught, he learned to play by watching players at the nearby public courts. He was 6'3" by the time he reached nineteen years old, and his height helped him develop a dominating serve that overpowered opponents.

Gonzales was ranked the best player in the world for a record eight years in a row. He won seventeen major singles titles over the course of his career, including two Grand Slams. When the editors of *Sports Illustrated* picked their favorite athletes of the twentieth century, they ranked Gonzales fifteenth, saying that if the fate of the earth was on the line in a tennis match, Gonzales would be the man humankind would want serving.

One of Gonzales's most unusual matches, though, was in 1969 against Charlie Pasarell at Wimbledon. Gonzales was a forty-one-year old at the time and a grandfather. Pasarell was not only much younger (twenty-five) but had trained under Gonzales, learning his technique by copying the older man's strokes.

The match started with each player holding his serve. When Gonzales served, Gonzales won the game. When Pasarell served, Pasarell won the game. This went back and forth. First for five games, then ten, then fifteen. Numerous times Gonzales saved set points to avoid defeat. Twenty games, then thirty, then forty. Finally, with a lob to the back edge of the baseline in the forty-sixth game, Pasarell broke Gonzales's serve. The first set was his, twenty-four games to twenty-two.

The second set began a little after seven p.m. It was a gloomy day in London and the light was fading. Gonzales complained about the deteriorating visibility, but the tournament referee ignored him. Whether because he was angry, or couldn't see, Gonzales lost again, but much faster this time, 1–6. Play was called after the end of the second set.

The next morning proved better weather, and the players

returned to the closely fought contest. Gonzales bent repeatedly but never broke, and the sets crept upward, 6–6, 8–8, and 10–10. Pasarell soon began to feel the pressure of trying to finish off his former mentor. After twenty-nine sets, Pasarell double faulted twice and lost the third set 14–16.

At this point the tide had begun to turn. Pasarell double-faulted again and lost the fourth set 3–6. Now the match was tied, two sets to two. Gonzales looked tired, leaning on his racquet between points and stalling for time. But he would not give up. Pasarell had him on the ropes time and time again, but couldn't push it through. Gonzales was serving at 4–5 down 0–40 but the lob shots that had worked so well for Pasarell earlier in the match began to falter. Gonzales fought back, and seven deuces later, he won to tie the score at 5–5.

Pasarell won the next game, but Gonzales again came from 0–40 to tie things at 6–6. Again the momentum shifted back and forth as the game tally went higher and higher. Eventually Gonzales won the final 11 points to win the set 11–9, and the match.

The contest had lasted more than 5 hours and spanned more than 110 games. It's one of the longest singles matches in the history of Wimbledon.

Based in part on this epic contest, Wimbledon introduced the tiebreak in 1971. Rather than playing game after game until someone gets ahead by two, for sets tied at six games each, a tie-break game determines the winner.* Players alternate serving and whoever scores 7 points first wins (as long as they have 2 points more than their opponent). Tiebreak games can still go on for a

---

* In all but the final set.

while, but they decrease the chance matches go on for as long as Gonzales and Pasarell did.

Similar to our work on basketball, an economist wondered how losing in tennis would affect performance.[20] Take a player who loses a tiebreak: Does that loss influence how well he plays the rest of the match?

After analyzing thousands of matches, he found that the answer was a resounding yes. But the impact is actually the opposite of what we found in basketball. Rather than leading players to do better, losing led tennis players to do *worse*. Players that lose a first-set tiebreak lose an extra game, on average, in the second set.

Why would that be?

It's tempting to attribute the differing impact of losing to distinctions between the two sports. Basketball is a team sport, while tennis is an individual one. Basketball games last less than an hour, while tennis matches often go on for two or three times as long. There are a number of other differences.

But it turns out that the disparity has less to do with distinctions between basketball and tennis and more to do with the size of the discrepancy, or how bad the losers were losing.

People get more motivated as they get closer to their goal. Take the cards you get at coffee shops, bagel stores, or as part of other loyalty programs. These cards reward frequent patronage with free stuff. Buy nine coffees, get the tenth free. Every sixth bagel is complimentary. Rewards like these encourage people to return to the store, but how motivating they are depends on how close people are to achieving the reward. Compared to people who have just started the card, people who have almost completed it buy much faster.[21] Feeling like we're almost there makes us more motivated, so we come back to the store sooner.

Animals show the same pattern of behavior.[22] Compared to rats that just started running a maze, those close to reaching a reward (cheese, for example) run faster. The closer they are, the more motivated they become.

In competition, then, it's not just about being behind. It's about *how far behind* someone is. Being down by a little is often more motivating than being down by a lot because people are closer to achieving their goal of winning.

Take a team losing by one point at halftime. They're almost there. They're just like the rat that runs around the corner and sees the cheese. If they play good defense, and hit an extra shot, they can close the gap. If they give just a little bit more effort, they can go from losing to winning. As a basketball announcer might say, they're so close they can almost taste it.

Compare that to a team that's further behind. Say, losing by 8 points. They're still in the game, but they're not almost there. They have to make a number of stops on defense, make a number of extra shots, and maybe even go on a run. There is a lot between them and winning. They may be able to smell winning, but they're too far away to taste it.

When we're further back, it's harder to muster that extra motivation. The team down by 8 would still like to win, but they are so far behind that winning seems less likely. And it's harder to encourage that extra effort if we're not sure it will make much of a difference.

Along these lines, social comparisons not only increase motivation, they can also decrease it.

Rather than being down by 8 points, imagine being down by 20 or 25. You're so far back that the chance of winning seems remote. So many things would have to go right for you to catch up that you doubt it's even possible. So you begin to give up. In situations where success starts to seem impossible, motivation decreases. Competition becomes demotivating.

And that's what happened to tennis players who lost the tie-break. Winning the match didn't become impossible, but it became a lot more difficult. For best-of-three set matches, two sets is enough to win. So someone who just lost the first set tiebreak went from being almost halfway to winning the match to being halfway to losing it. They're not just behind by a little, they're behind by a lot.[*]

This rapid shift in relative performance should be particularly demotivating. Sure, being behind doesn't feel good, but it feels particularly bad when you were almost ahead by a bunch and then lost it. It's like thinking you're the top choice to be promoted and then finding out you're actually at the bottom of the list. Being at the bottom never feels good, but it's particularly bad when the top seemed oh, so close.[**]

---

[*] It's worth noting that research on Opower doesn't find a demotivating effect of being far behind (Allcott, 2011). Households that are told that their neighbors use much less energy than they do don't seem to give up and decide they no longer care about energy use. If anything, the data shows that the biggest energy hogs are the ones who conserve the most. People who used much more energy than others show the biggest decrease once the program is introduced. It's not clear, however, whether this is a psychological effect or a more mechanical one. Just as it's easier to lose two pounds if you're 20 pounds overweight than if you're only 3 pounds overweight, households that use more energy simply have more slack to trim. They also may not have taken as many steps yet to reduce consumption, and as a result it may just be easier for them to cut back.

[**] Winning can also be demotivating, but for a different reason. When someone is far ahead of their competition, being crowned the victor almost seems a certainty. Something drastic would have to happen for them to lose. Consequently, people take their foot off the gas pedal. Rather than

Not surprisingly, being too far behind can also lead people to quit.[23] To give up and stop trying altogether.

But interestingly, being far behind others isn't the only reason people quit. Quitting also depends on how well people expected to do compared to others in the first place.

In tennis, one player is often designated the favorite. They are ranked higher based on their recent performance in other matches. Similarly, compared to an upstart no one has ever heard of, most people expect an incumbent politician to win (as long as his or her tenure in office has been good).

But while favorites *should* perform better, this expectation often brings along additional baggage. People expect them to do well and this makes the potential of losing (and violating those expectations) even worse. If an underdog loses, it doesn't reflect that badly on the underdog. They were expected to lose, so losing doesn't change how people see them. But if the favorite loses, it has a more negative impact on others' impressions. They were expected to win, and anything less signals that the favorite might not have been so great after all.

Consequently, competitors may search for a way to self-handicap. An excuse in the event of poor performance.

Someone worried about blowing a big presentation, for example,

---

continuing to work hard, they become complacent and coast. In Aesop's famous fable about the tortoise and the hare, for example, the hare dashes out in front of the tortoise and looks like it will easily win the race. But the hare is so confident of winning that he takes a nap. And by the time he has woken up, the tortoise has already won.

Note, however, that complacency should only kick in when the lead is decently sized. Being ahead by a little is unlikely to make people complacent.

might paradoxically stay out late the night before because it creates a handy external attribution for failure. If the presentation goes badly, he has an excuse. Rather than indicating something about their ability, there is now another explanation for any potential failure: *If I hadn't been out late, I would have done just fine.*

Quitting serves a similar function. Rather than sticking it out and losing, quitting allows competitors to preserve the notion that if they had just kept going, they would have won. That they were actually the stronger competitor, even though it didn't play out that way in the end.

Researchers found that favorites are more likely to quit for exactly this reason.[24] Compared to underdogs, tennis players favored to win were more likely to quit mid-match. Players who were ranked higher going in were more likely to throw in the towel, both literally and figuratively, particularly if they lost the first set.

For players who were supposed to win, but now looked like they might actually lose, quitting became a way to save face.

People and organizations often drop out of competitions. Basketball players pull up lame after shooting a jumper and sit out the rest of the game. Politicians drop out of the race to spend more time with their families. Companies take their name out of consideration for a contract to focus on other strategic priorities.

In some cases, quitting is warranted. The player hurt their leg, the politician loves their family, and the contract just wasn't in line with where the company saw its business going.

But in other cases, quitting provides a clever defense mechanism that enables people to avoid failure. It allows us to preserve the notion that we could have been successful if we had tried.

That if we had just kept competing, and pushed through it, we would have emerged victorious.

PUTTING SOCIAL INFLUENCE TO WORK

Where do these thoughts lead? Whether trying to inspire a sales team to work harder or encourage students to learn more, social comparisons can be a powerful motivating force. Giving people a sense of how they stack up against their peers can encourage them to work harder and be more likely to achieve their goals. At the same time, though, if not carefully designed, social comparisons can lead people to get disheartened, give up, and quit.

Unfortunately, many companies and classrooms use a winner-take-all model. The person who makes the most sales this quarter gets promoted. The top student is named valedictorian and speaks at graduation.

While this strategy motivates people who have a chance at the top slot, it often demotivates those who feel they have no shot at winning. Someone who has only half as many sales as the leader may think they are so far back that they just give up. Students that are getting Cs or Ds may feel similarly. Getting an A seems impossible, so why keep trying?

One way to encourage perseverance is to shrink the comparison set. Breaking larger groups up into smaller ones based on performance. Golf tournaments organize participants into groups of similar skill. This encourages golfers to compare themselves to others of similar ability, which decreases the chance they feel far behind and helps maintain motivation.

Similarly, rather than comparing people to everyone else, some organizations give people feedback that compares them to the person just ahead of them. Opower doesn't compare people to their best-performing neighbor, they tell people where they are in relation to neighbors with similar homes. Just like basketball teams that were down by a point, making each person feel slightly behind increases effort and performance.

Social comparisons can also be made to other classes or firms. Rental car company Avis, for example, used to claim that they tried harder because they were number two rather than number one. Harvard professor Todd Rogers and UC Berkeley professor Don Moore tested a version of this idea in politics. They sent out e-mails to more than a million Florida Democrats suggesting that their gubernatorial candidate was either winning or losing by a little in the polls. Emphasizing that the candidate was behind raised 60 percent more money.[25] Thinking their candidate was losing by a little motivated people to do something about it.

These ideas even have implications for whom to hire. Picking someone who is qualified, but for whom the job is a slight stretch, often nets more motivated individuals. When looking for state directors, for example, President Obama's 2008 campaign preferred to pick someone who had previously been a deputy director, rather than someone who had been a director many times already. Not only were these folks cheaper, but it created a group of individuals who had something to prove. They saw themselves as slightly behind, and were more motivated and less likely to be complacent.[26]

When it comes to hiring, raising money, or even conserving energy, people aren't rational robots. Where they stand in relation to others affects motivation.

Social facilitation can also help people reach their personal best. Whether training for a half marathon or just trying to lose a couple pounds, peers are a useful tool to help increase success.

At a basic level, peers provide a useful commitment device. Most people mean to exercise at least a few times a week, but it's easy for work, family, and life to get in the way. It's harder to skip a workout, though, when someone else is waiting for you. Planning to meet a friend at the gym at 6:30 p.m. increases the chance we follow through.

Peers can also motivate people to work harder. When we're by ourselves, it's easy to slack off. We often mean to do a few sets of certain exercises, but if the first couple were harder than expected, it's easy to convince ourselves that two is more than enough.

It's harder to give in when someone else is there. Just like the cockroaches running in the stadium, people often exert more effort when others are around. Particularly if we're competitive, working out with friends can push us to go further, faster, and harder than we would otherwise. Even if you're not competitive, simply having others around will encourage you to stick to what you planned.

If it's hard to find a workout partner, run, or go to the gym when others are around. Pick the treadmill next to another runner rather than one that is far away. Their mere presence should encourage us to give it 110 percent.*

---

* Two caveats. First, avoid direct comparison with others who are of much higher ability. A professional runner can give great tips, but going running with them all the time might make people feel so far behind that they give up. Picking someone who is a little bit better or a little bit worse is a better idea. If they are a little better, that will motivate us to work harder. And if they are a little worse, at least it will make us feel good about ourselves.

Second, be careful involving others when just getting started. If someone has never shot a basketball before, other people can provide pointers, but they may also increase anxiety. Learning from someone we know well should reduce any potential negative impact.

Conclusion:
Putting Social Influence to Work

America has always been seen as the land of opportunity. But the reality that immigrants encountered was often far from that lofty ideal. In the early 1900s, new arrivals to New York City often slept twelve to a room in teetering tenements. Street children huddled together over grates for warmth or roamed the alleyways as shoeshines and beggars. The slums were a chaotic mess of poverty and desolation, mixed with a dash of hope. Dilapidated wooden shacks, packed together, that could easily be mistaken for today's developing world.

Spurred on by these conditions, in the 1930s the United States began to develop public housing. As part of Franklin Roosevelt's New Deal, the National Industrial Recovery Act directed the Public Works Administration to clear the slums and construct low-income dwellings. The first public housing project opened in Atlanta in 1936, and by the end of the decade, more than fifty additional projects had been built all across America.

Renowned architects were commissioned to design communities that fostered interaction. Buildings were constructed with central spaces for children to play and complexes included libraries and kindergartens on-site. Some units even had their own bathtubs and electric ranges, luxuries at that time.

These developments were intended to eliminate the slums, but many soon became slums themselves. Physical deterioration and backlogged repairs led to mold and vandalism. Cockroaches ran rampant. Shoddy construction and mismanagement led to general dissatisfaction and high vacancy rates.

Originally built with high standards and catering to a wide range of applicants, public housing eventually became a last resort. It came to stand for concentrated poverty, crime, and racial segregation. Politicians resisted the creation of units in middle- and working-class neighborhoods, focusing construction around already poor areas of the city. White flight from the inner city to suburbia and income requirements further segregated the population. Soon the only individuals left in public housing were people who didn't have anywhere else to go.

Starting in the late 1960s and early 1970s, the government tried a different approach. Rather than focusing on supply, or the number of low-cost units being built, the Experimental Housing Allowance Program focused on the demand side as well. Instead of just providing "project-based" assistance that applied to the development of specific properties, individual households were given vouchers. This tenant-based support covered the gap between 25 percent of a household's income and fair market rent and could be used anywhere vouchers were accepted. No longer constrained to the projects, people were free to move wherever they pleased.

Vouchers were designed to encourage people to move to better areas. The idea was that low-income families now had a choice. Rather than being forced to concentrate in the projects, they could move to regions with less crime and poverty.

Unfortunately, however, many didn't. It turned out that the problem was about more than just flexibility. Households receiving rental assistance were confronted with an array of other barriers. Lack of information about other potential locations, discrimination, market conditions, and lack of transportation conspired to keep individuals localized in communities of intense poverty. Even when it seemed like they could go elsewhere, they couldn't.

In 1992, the U.S. government created a new program called Moving to Opportunity. Recognizing the difficulties with prior efforts, the program combined rental assistance vouchers with intensive housing search and counseling services. Giving people the ability to move, paired with the support to make it happen.

The initial effort was restricted to sizable cities situated in larger metropolitan areas. Of the twenty-one possible U.S. locations, a competitive process whittled the list down to five: Baltimore, Boston, Chicago, New York, and Los Angeles.

In each city, the local public housing administration recruited participants through fliers, tenant associations, and a variety of other means. Participation was limited to low-income families with children. Families had to be living in either public housing or Section 8 project-based housing located in poor areas. Places where the poverty rate was at least 40 percent. Three-quarters of applicants were on welfare and less than half had graduated from high school.

Demand was high, so participation was determined by lottery. And, consistent with the program's name, Moving to Opportunity didn't just encourage people to move, it encouraged them to move to lower-poverty communities. Applicants received counseling and assistance finding a private unit to lease, but the unit had to be somewhere with less than 10 percent of the population below the poverty line. These low-income families couldn't just move from one project to another, the program encouraged them to move from what tended to be some of America's most distressed urban neighborhoods to a completely different environment.

This aspect of Moving to Opportunity was particularly important. For decades, scientists and policy makers have debated the impact of what have been termed "neighborhood effects." People who live in high-poverty areas tend to fare worse on a variety of dimensions.[1] Children who grow up in poorer neighborhoods tend to have lower IQs, verbal ability, and reading scores. Adolescents are more likely to drop out of school, display aggression, and commit crimes. There are higher rates of depression, joblessness, alcohol abuse, and mental health issues. Across a wide range of economic, health, and educational outcomes, people from poorer neighborhoods are worse off.

The cause of this disparity, however, is less clear. People who grow up in poorer neighborhoods certainly face greater challenges. Crime is already high, schools are underfunded, and government services are lower quality. Racial segregation is high. There are fewer high-paying jobs and more hurdles to overcome to get them.

But family characteristics like income, race, and education also vary. The people who live in poorer neighborhoods are not exactly the same as the people who live in wealthier ones.

Consequently, it is hard to determine what's driving the disparity. Is it individual and family circumstances or the effect of the neighborhood itself? Do children who grow up in poor neighborhoods tend to do worse in school because the schools are bad or because their parents are less educated? Do people who live in high-poverty areas tend to have more behavioral and mental health problems because of who they are or where they live?

It's a classic question of nature versus nurture. How much are life outcomes driven by genetics versus the environment? By who people are, versus what surrounds them?[2]

The answer has important policy implications. Should the government pay for more tutoring programs or enable poor families to move to higher-income areas? Focus on individual health or on improving communities?

The Moving to Opportunity program provided a unique chance to investigate these questions. By randomly giving some families the opportunity to move to better neighborhoods, while others stayed put, scientists could examine how neighborhoods affect outcomes. Nurture, not nature.

Years later, when scientists analyzed the data, they found some impressive effects. Moving to lower-poverty areas greatly improved the health and well-being of both children and adults.[3] Not only were kids 35 percent less likely to be victims of a crime, they were less likely to be injured or have asthma attacks. Girls were less likely to use marijuana and less likely to be arrested for property crime. Adults were less likely to be obese, experience psychological distress, or experience clinical depression. Moving had as big an effect in decreasing diabetes likelihood as taking diabetes medication.

The most striking effects, though, were on economic outcomes.[4] Children whose families moved to a lower-poverty neighborhood before they turned thirteen were more likely to attend college and had higher-earning jobs later in life. As adults, these children ended up living in better neighborhoods themselves and were less likely to become single parents.

And the effects were sizable. When followed up with in their mid-twenties, compared to children who didn't move, those who did were earning almost 33 percent more a year than their peers.*

Effects were even larger for children who moved at a younger age. Children who moved at age eight were expected to earn more than $300,000 over the course of their careers.[5] This boost more than paid for the incremental cost of the subsidized voucher.

Moving to better neighborhoods improved people's lives, and the longer they lived in those better neighborhoods, the more their lives improved.

Where we live has a big impact on how our lives unfold.

Neighborhood effects are certainly multifaceted. Environments can encourage better health and well-being for a variety of reasons. Some areas have more produce-filled grocery stores, lower student-to-teacher ratios, and more community centers

---

* Related research examined exactly how much growing up in different areas either increased or decreased expected income later in life. Each additional year spent growing up in Bergen, New Jersey, for example, raises household income in adulthood by around 0.70 percent. Each additional year spent in Manhattan, New York, however, decreases later household income by over 0.50 percent. This may not seem huge by itself, but it creates sizable differences when aggregated across twenty years of exposure. Growing up in Bergen would raise earnings by almost 15 percent relative to the national average, while growing up in New York City would decrease earnings by almost 10 percent. See http://www.equality-of-opportunity.org/ for more information.

where kids can run and play. All of which should lead to happier, healthier, and more prosperous residents.

But another key aspect is other people. One's peers. Are they playing sports or watching television? Are they joining the debate team or doing drugs?

And whether you're a kid growing up in a poor neighborhood, or a business executive living in a wealthy one, others surround us every day. The kids next door. Our coworkers at the office. The person swimming in the lane next to us at the pool.

Do our environments determine our fate? Certainly not. Growing up poor is no more of a life sentence than growing up rich is a guarantee.

But we are constantly shaped by the people around us.

Sometimes social influence leads to imitation. Like monkeys choosing between red and blue corn, we use others' behavior as information, simplifying choice and allowing us to pick better (and tastier) things than we might have on our own. We mimic the choices and actions of peers, and such imitation determines everything from how we look to the products and ideas that catch on.

That said, others not only attract, they can also repel. We order a different beverage than our dining companion or abandon music artists once they become too popular. Like younger siblings differentiating themselves from older ones, we strive to craft a distinct, separable identity. Even if we don't always choose differently, we frame our choices in ways that allow us to feel different enough.

And whether we imitate or differentiate depends on *who* those others are. The choices we make—what we wear, how hard we try in school, and what career we pursue—depend on who else is doing those things. Like small green frogs, we pick things that send desired signals, and avoid choices and actions that send undesired ones.

But it's not simply either/or. We don't want to be exactly the same or completely different. Instead, we choose and behave in ways that allow us to be optimally distinct, threading the needle between similarity and difference. Like Goldilocks, we avoid the extremes. We like things that are moderately similar, blending the allure of novelty with the comfort of the familiar until it feels just right.

Finally, peers don't just affect what we choose, they motivate us to action. Others make us bike faster, save more energy, and turn losing into winning. And yet, if we fall too far behind, those same others can lead us to quit. To give up because the gap seems too large.

But even though others shape almost everything we do, we are often unaware that this impact occurs. We can all point to examples of others falling prey to social influence, but it's often much harder to recognize that influence on ourselves.

Early in the book, we read about an experiment involving college students' judgments of physical attractiveness. Psychologist Richard Moreland found that students who came to class more often were seen as more attractive. Seeing someone more often made people like them more.

Years earlier, when Moreland was in college, he worked at the local grocery store called Joyce's in Boulder, Colorado, just like the imaginary couple we met in the introduction. A young girl worked there at the same time, and after seeing her a few times, Moreland realized that he found her quite cute. They talked, then dated, and eventually this coworker became his wife.

The store was actually a hotbed of romance. Almost all the employees ended up marrying each other. Between school and work, people didn't have much time to meet anyone else, so they ended up loving the one they were with.

Did seeing this woman more often make Moreland like her more, and eventually marry her as a result?

As each of us would do when asked such a question, Moreland would say no. We prefer to think that we were attracted to our partner because they are charming or have a nice smile, not because we happened to have the same work schedules.

Just as with the products we buy and the career we choose, we believe that we consciously choose our spouse and our friends. That we select them based on our personal preferences, not based on how many times we happened to see them or who else they were associated with.

And yet, as an outsider looking at someone else's behavior, it's hard not to wonder.

Because, at our core, we are all social animals. Whether we realize it or not, other people have a subtle and surprising impact on almost everything we do. When it comes to our own lives, social influence is as silent as it is powerful. Just because we can't see it, it doesn't mean it's not there.

It's easy to see social influence with a cynical eye and bemoan that people are lemmings. Mindless followers swayed by those around them. And there are certainly cases where conformity is bad. Our tendency to imitate can encourage us to go along when we should dissent, or stay silent when we should speak up.

But, by itself, social influence is neither bad nor good. If people follow others who are evil, it will lead to more evil in the world. If people follow others that are good, it will lead to more good.

We can also choose our influence. Social influence has a huge impact on behavior. But by understanding how it works, we can harness its power. We can avoid its downsides and take advantage of its benefits. We can maintain our individuality and avoid being swept up in the crowd. We can have more fulfilling social interactions, be more successful, and use others to help us make better-informed decisions. By understanding when social influence is beneficial, we can decide when to resist influence and when to embrace it.

By gaining insight into how social influence works, we can put it to work, improving our own lives, and the lives of others. Influence is a tool, like any other. If we understand it, we don't have to stand passively by and just watch it happen. We can use it. We can design environments, shape situations, and build programs like Opower and Moving to Opportunity that harness the power of social influence to make the world a better place.

Where do you see influence? How do the others around you shape your life and how are you shaping theirs?

Understanding these often invisible influences can make us all better off.

Want to be more influential? Make better decisions?
Motivate yourself and others?

Get more tips and tools at JonahBerger.com

Acknowledgments

In some ways, writing the Acknowledgments section of a second book is tougher than the first. If you're not sure you'll ever write another book, you spend the first book thanking all the people that have helped you on your journey throughout life. If you end up writing a second book, though, you're a little stuck. Should you re-thank all the people that helped you get there? Is thanking them the first time around enough? Regardless, another thanks to all the people I mentioned in *Contagious: Why Things Catch On*. Without you, *Invisible Influence* would not have been possible.

Many new thanks as well. Thanks to Tanya Chartrand, Sapna Cheryan, and Sarah Townsend for helpful research pointers along the way, Rebecca Bruno for sharing insights on baby names, and Richard Moreland, Nicole Stephens, and a number of other people who didn't end up making the final version for generously agreeing to be interviewed. Thanks to Ben Loehnen, Richard Rhorer, Maureen Cole, and the rest of the team at Simon & Schuster for making this book just as fun to work on as the last one, Alice La Plante for sharpening the writing, and the eagle-eyed Mara Ana Vitorino for editing, even while pregnant. Thanks to all the players and staff at East Palo Alto AYSO for allowing me to coach, the Marketing faculty at Duke University for lending me an office while I wrote much of this book, and guys from pickup basketball at Wilson for giving me a great break from writing. I am terrible, but hopefully this book provides a reasonable excuse.

A huge debt of gratitude goes out to both my collaborators and anyone whose research is mentioned in this book. Being a social scientist would not be anywhere near as fun without you. My journey into social psychology started in Eliot Applestein's AP psychology course in high school. My final paper for that class ended up being about groupthink, and it got me started thinking about how social influence impacts behavior. Thanks to him and all the other teachers and professors along the way—Lee Ross, Mark Lepper, Hazel Markus, and Phil Zimbardo, and various others that took the time to share the wonder of the field with me. I feel lucky to be a part of it.

Someone once asked a group of people who their favorite social psychologist was. It's an impossible question to answer. In addition to the giants mentioned above, Cialdini, Lewin, Sherif, and others would certainly be on my list. But in terms of sheer breadth of contribution, Bob Zajonc would certainly be up there. It's amazing how many studies in this book reference his work and how many areas he contributed to. Learning his life story only adds to the legend.

Thanks again to Jim Levine. The longer we work together the more I appreciate everything you do. You always give sage advice and provide a great reminder that a fulfilling life lived is about more than just work. Thanks also to Diane and Jeffrey, Nancy and Steve, Kiva, Victor, Danny, Fred, and all the other people that took the time to lead the way and provide encouragement. In addition to the requested feedback, you always provide an extra dose of enthusiasm to keep me going.

And most importantly, to Jordan and Zoë. For helping and supporting, cajoling and understanding, listening and thinking, and caring and believing every step of the way. Even when we all agree that chasing a tennis ball would be much more fun. Your influence is both visible and invisible, and for both I am sincerely grateful.

Notes

Introduction

1. The literature on social influence is huge, but for some examples, see Sorensen, Alan T. (2006), "Social Learning and Health Plan Choice," *RAND Journal of Economics* 37, 929–45; Sacerdote, Bruce (2001), "Peer Effects with Random Assignment: Results for Dartmouth Roommates," *Quarterly Journal of Economics* 116, 681–704; Lerner, Josh, and Ulrike Malmendier (2013), "With a Little Help from My (Random) Friends: Success and Failure in Post-Business School Entrepreneurship," *Review of Financial Studies* 26, 2411–52; Beshears, John, J. Choi, D. Laibson, B. C. Madrian, and K. L. Milkman (2012), "The Effect of Providing Peer Information on Retirement Savings Decisions," *Financial Literacy Center Working Paper,* WR- 800-SSA; Case, Anne, and Lawrence Katz (1991), "The Company You Keep: The Effects of Family and Neighborhood on Disadvantaged Youths," *National Bureau of Economic Research Working Paper Number 3705;* Brown, Jeffrey, Z. Ivkovic, P. Smith, and S. Weisbenner (2008), "Neighbors Matter: Causal Community Effects and Stock Market Participation,"*Journal of Finance* 63, 1509–31; Gerber, Alan, and Todd Rogers (2009), "Descriptive Social Norms and Motivation to Vote: Everybody's Voting and So Should You," *Journal of Politics* 71, 1–14; Frey, Bruno, and Stephan Meier (2004), "Social Comparisons and Pro-Social Behavior: Testing 'Conditional Cooperation' in a Field Experiment,"*American Economic Review* 94, 1717–22; and Card, D., A. Mas, E. Moretti, and

E. Saez (2012), "Inequality at Work: The Effect of Peer Salaries on Job Satisfaction," *American Economic Review* 10, 2981–3003.

2. Pronin, Emily, Jonah Berger, and Sarah Molouki (2007), "Alone in a Crowd of Sheep: Asymmetric Perceptions of Conformity and Their Roots in an Introspection Illusion," *Journal of Personality and Social Psychology* 92, 585–95.

3. To control for order effects, we randomized the order of the questions. Sometimes people answered the questions about their own purchase first and then someone else's. Other times people completed the questions for someone else's purchase and then rated their own.

4. Match.com and Chadwick Martin Bailey Behavioral Studies (2010), "Match.com and Chadwick Martin Bailey 2009–2010 Studies: Recent Trends: Online Dating," 1–5.

5. For a review of mere exposure research, see Bornstein, Robert (1989), "Exposure and Affect: Overview and Meta-Analysis of Research," *Psychological Bulletin* 106, 263–89.

1. Monkey See, Monkey Do

1. Sherif, Muzafer (1935), "A Study of Some Social Factors in Perception: Chapter 2," *Archives of Psychology* 187, 17–22.

2. For a summary of some of Asch's studies, see Asch, Solomon (1956), "Studies of Independence and Conformity: A Minority of One Against a Unanimous Majority," *Psychological Monographs* 70, 1–70.

3. Waal, Erica, C. Borgeaud, and A. Whiten (2013), "Potent Social Learning and Conformity Shape a Wild Primate's Foraging Decisions," *Science* 340, 483–85. Other animal research shows that whales acquire new feeding methods from other whales. See Allen, Jenny, M. Weinrich, W. Hoppitt, and L. Rendell (2013), "Network-Based Diffusion Analysis Reveals Cultural Transmission of Lobtail Feeding in Humpback Whales," *Science* 26, 485–88; and Dindo, Marietta, T. Stoinski, and A. Whiten (2011), "Observational Learning in Orangutan Cultural Transmission Chains," *Biology Letters* 7, 181–83. Other work suggests that different groups of chimpanzees have different cultures, which is consistent with the notion that they learn from others in their own group but that different groups differ. See Whiten, Andrew, J. Goodall, W. McGrew, T. Nishida, V. Reynolds, Y. Sugiyama, and C. Boesch (1999), "Cultures in Chimpanzees," *Nature* 399, 682–85. Fish copy other fish. See Pike, Thomas, and Kevin Laland (2010), "Conformist Learning in Nine-Spined Sticklebacks' Foraging Decisions," *Biology Letters* 6, 466–68.

4. Little, Anthony C., Michael Burt, and David Perrett (2006), "Assortative Mating for Perceived Facial Personality Traits," *Personality and Individual Differences* 40, 973–84; Hinsz, Verlin (1989), "Facial Resemblance in Engaged and Married Couples," *Journal of Social and Personal Relationships* 6, 223–29; Griffiths, Wayne, and Phillip Kunz (1973), "Assortative Mating: A Study of Physiognomic Homogamy," *Social Biology* 20, 448–53; Zajonc, Robert, Pamela Adelmann, Sheila Murphy, and Paula Niedenthal (1987), "Convergence in the Physical Appearance of Spouses," *Motivation and Emotion* 11, 335–46.

5. Turns out there are many reasons chameleons change color, including temperature, light, and mood. While many of these have nothing to do with the color of their surroundings, popular perception remains that chameleons change to fit their environment. Ligon, Russell, and The Conversation (2013), "Chameleons Talk Tough by Changing Colors," The Conversation (December 19), reposted at http://www.scientificamerican.com/article/chameleons-talk-tough-by-changing-colors/.

6. Chartrand, Tanya, and John Bargh (1999), "The Chameleon Effect: The Perception-Behavior Link and Social Interaction," *Journal of Personality and Social Psychology* 76, 893–910. For integrative reviews of research on mimicry, see Van Baaren, Rick, L. Jansen, T. Chartrand, and A. Dijksterhuis (2009), "Where Is the Love? The Social Aspects of Mimicry," *Philosophical Transactions of the Royal Society* 364, 2381–89; and Chartrand, Tanya, and Jessica Lakin (2013), "The Antecedents and Consequences of Human Behavioral Mimicry," *Annual Review of Psychology* 64, 285–308.

7. Simner, Marvin (1971), "Newborn's Response to the Cry of Another Infant," *Developmental Psychology* 5, 136–50.

8. Mirror Neuron Forum (2011), *Perspectives on Psychological Science* 6, 369–407.

9. For an early discussion of mirror neurons, see Fadiga, L., L. Fogassi, G. Pavesi, and G. Rizzolatti (1995), "Motor Facilitation During Action Observation: A Magnetic Stimulation Study," *Journal of Neurophysiology* 73, 2608–11. For a more recent discussion, see Gallese, Vittorio, M. Gernsbacher, C. Hayes, G. Hickok, and M. Iacoboni (2011), "Mirror Neuron Forum," *Perspectives on Psychological Science* 6, 369–407.

10. Maddux, W. W., E. Mullen, and A. Galinsky (2008), "Chameleons Bake Bigger Pies and Take Bigger Pieces: Strategic Behavioral

Mimicry Facilitates Negotiation Outcomes," *Journal of Experimental Social Psychology* 44, 461–68.

11. For some examples of the consequences of mimicry, see Ireland, Molly, R. Slatcher, P. Eastwick, L. Scissors, E. Finkel, and J. Pennebaker (2010), "Language Style Matching Predicts Relationship Initiation and Stability," *Psychological Science* 20, 1–6; Maddux et al., "Chameleons Bake Bigger Pies and Take Bigger Pieces"; and Van Baaren, Rick, R. Holland, B. Steenaert, and A. Knippenberg (2003), "Mimicry for Money: Behavioral Consequences of Imitation," *Journal of Experimental Social Psychology* 39, 393–98.

12. Sorensen, Alan (2007), "Bestseller Lists and Product Variety," *Journal of Industrial Economics* 4, 715–38.

2. A Horse of a Different Color

1. LeBolt, Dr. Wendy (2014), "Are National Team Players Born or Made?" SoccerWire.com (December 2).

2. Hopwood, Melissa J., J. Baker, C. MacMahon, and D. Farrow (2012), "Faster, Higher, Stronger . . . and Younger? Birth Order, Sibling Sport Participation and Sport Expertise," paper presented at the North American Society for the Psychology of Sport and Physical Activity Conference, Honolulu, Hawaii (June 2012), *Journal of Sport & Exercise Psychology* 34, S235.

3. There is a great deal of research on birth order and academic achievement, but for some examples, see Zajonc, Robert, and Gregory Markus (1975), "Birth Order and Intellectual Development," *Psychological Review* 82, 74–88; Zajonc, Robert (2001), "The Family Dynamics of Intellectual Development," *American Psychologist* 56, 490–96; Zajonc, Robert (1976), "Family Configuration and Intelligence," *Science* 16, 227–36; Hotz, Joseph, and Juan Pantano (2013), "Strategic Parenting, Birth Order, and School Performance," *Journal of Population Economics,* 1–26; Behrman, Jere, and Paul Taubman (1986), "Birth Order, Schooling and Earnings," *Journal of Labor Economics* 4, S121–S145; Black, Sandra, P. Devereux, and K. Salvanes (2005), "The More the Merrier? The Effect of Family Size and Birth Order on Children's Education," *Quarterly Journal of Economics* 120, 669–700; and Black, Sandra, P. Devereux, and K. Salvanes (2008), "Small Family, Smart Family? Family Size and the IQ Scores of Young Men," *National Bureau of Economic Research Working Paper No. 13336.*

4. Paulhaus, Delroy, P. Trapnell, and D. Chen (1999), "Birth Order Effects on Personality and Achievement Within Families," *Psychological Science* 10, 482–88.

5. Altus, William (1966), "Birth Order and Its Sequelae," *Science* 151, 44–49; Clark, Roger, and Glenn Rice (1982), "Family Constellations and Eminence: The Birth Orders of Nobel Prize winners," *Journal of Psychology* 110, 281–87; and Sulloway, Frank (1996), *Born to Rebel: Birth Order, Family Dynamics, and Creative Lives* (New York: Vintage Books).

6. Theroux, N. L. (1993), "Birth Order and Its Relationship to Academic Achievement and Selected Personal Traits." unpublished doctoral dissertation, University of California, Los Angeles.

7. Ibid.

8. Sulloway, Frank (2010), "Why Siblings Are Like Darwin's Finches: Birth Order, Sibling Competition, and Adaptive Divergence Within the Family," in *The Evolution of Personality and Individual Differences*, eds. David M. Buss and Patricia H. Hawley (New York: Oxford University Press), 86–119; Plomin, Robert, and Denise Daniels (1987), "Why Are Children in the Same Family So Different from One Another?" *Behavioral and Brain Sciences* 10, 1–16.

9. The question of how much siblings' personalities are driven by shared environmental influences is an ongoing area of research. While some researchers find little evidence of shared environmental influences, others find some evidence that it exists. Regardless of the exact influence of shared environment, however, what is clear is that even growing up with the same genetic makeup, in the same household, with the same parents, can lead two people to come out drastically different. And desires for differentiation likely play at least some role in this process. Even if people merely perceive their brothers and sisters as different from them, this provides some evidence for the desire to differentiate oneself from one's siblings. See Matteson, Lindsay, M. McGue, and W. Iacono (2013), "Shared Environmental Influences on Personality: A Combined Twin and Adoption Approach," *Behavior Genetics* 43, 491–504; and Borkenau, Peter, R. Riemann, A. Angleitner, and M. Spinath (2001), "Genetic and Environmental Influences on Observed Personality: Evidence from the German Observational Study of Adult Twins," *Journal of Personality and Social Psychology* 80, 655–68.

10. Loehlin, John (1992), *Genes and Environment in Personality Development* (Newbury Park, CA: Sage).

11. Loehlin, John, J. Horn, and L. Willerman (1981), "Personality Resemblance in Adoptive Families," *Behavior Genetics* 11, 309–30.

12. Schachter, F. F., G. Gilutz, E. Shore, and M. Adler (1978), "Sibling Deidentification Judged by Mothers: Cross-Validation and Developmental Studies," *Child Development* 49, 543–46.

13. Loehlin, John, J. Horn, and L. Willerman (1990), "Heredity, Environment, and Personality Change: Evidence from the Texas Adoption Project," *Journal of Personality* 58, 221–43.

14. Ariely, Dan, and Jonathan Leavav (2000), "Sequential Choice in Group Settings: Taking the Road Less Traveled and Less Enjoyed," *Journal of Consumer Research* 27, 279–90.

15. DeVito, Carlo (2008), *Yogi: The Life & Times of an American Original* (Chicago: Triumph Books).

16. Howe, Daniel (1988), *The Impact of Puritanism on American Culture* (New York: Charles Scribner's Sons).

17. De Tocqueville, Alexis (2003), *Democracy in America* (New York: Penguin).

18. Tian, Kelly T., William O. Bearden, and Gary L. Hunter (2001), "Consumers' Need for Uniqueness: Scale Development and Validation," *Journal of Consumer Research* 28, 50–66; and Simonson, Itamar, and Stephen M. Nowlis (2000), "The Role of Explanations and Need for Uniqueness in Consumer Decision Making: Unconventional Choices Based on Reasons," *Journal of Consumer Research* 27, 49–68.

19. Semertzidis, Konstantinos, E. Pitoura, and P. Tsaparas (2013), "How People Describe Themselves on Twitter," Association for Computing Machinery: Proceedings of the ACM SIGMOD Workshop on Databases and Social Networks, New York, NY (June 22, 2013).

20. People with unusual first names, firstborn or only children, children of interfaith marriages, and women whose nearest sibling is male rather than female all have greater desires for differentiation. Salient or unique personal attributes may lead people to see themselves as different, which in turn makes distinction seem desirable. Snyder, Charles, and Shane J. Lopez (2002), "Uniqueness Seeking," *Handbook of Positive Psychology* 18, 395–410.

21. Heejung, Kim, and Hazel Markus (1999), "Deviance or Uniqueness, Harmony or Conformity? A Cultural Analysis," *Journal of Personality and Social Psychology* 77, 785–800.

22. Kusserow, Adrie (1999), "De-Homogenizing American Individualism: Socializing Hard and Soft Individualism in Manhattan and Queens," *Ethos* 27, 210–34; and Wiley, Angela, A. Rose, L. Burger, P. Miller (1998), "Constructing Autonomous Selves Through

Narrative Practices: A Comparative Study of Working-class and Middle-class Families," *Child Development* 69, 833–47.

23. For research on how working-class contexts shape behavior, see Argyle, Michael (1994), *The Psychology of Social Class* (London: Routledge); Markus, Hazel, C. Ryff, K. Curhan, and K. Palmersheim (2004), "In Their Own Words: Well-being at Midlife Among High School–Educated and College-Educated Adults," in *How Healthy Are We? A National Study of Well-being at Midlife*, eds. Orville Gilbert Brim, Carol D. Ryff, and Ronald C. Kessler (Chicago: University of Chicago Press), 273–319; Lamont, Michèle (2000), *The Dignity of Working Men: Morality and the Boundaries of Race, Class, and Immigration* (Cambridge, MA: Harvard University Press); Kohn, Melvin, and Carmi Schooler (1986), "Work and Personality: An Inquiry into the Impact of Social Stratification," *Political Psychology* 7, 605–7; and Miller, Peggy, G. Cho, and J. Bracey (2005), "Working-class Children's Experience Through the Prism of Personal Storytelling," *Human Development* 48, 115–35.

24. Stephens, Nicole, H. Markus, and S. Townsend (2007), "Choice as an Act of Meaning: The Case of Social Class," *Journal of Personality and Social Psychology* 93, 814–30.

3. Not If *They're* Doing It

1. Baran, S. J., J. J. Mok, M. Land, and T. Y. Kang (1989), "You Are What You Buy: Mass-Mediated Judgments of People's Worth," *Journal of Communication* 39, 46–54. For a great review of research on how people make inferences based on everything from clothes to websites, see Gosling, Sam (2008), *Snoop: What Your Stuff Says About You* (New York: Basic Books).

2. For some early work on signaling in economics, see Spence, Michael (1973), "Job Market Signaling," *The Quarterly Journal of Economics* 87, 355–74.

3. Cohen, Geoffrey L. (2003), "Party Over Policy: The Dominating Impact of Group Influence on Political Beliefs," *Journal of Personality and Social Psychology* 85, 808–22.

4. Bee, Mark, S. Perrill, and P. Owen (2000), "Male Green Frogs Lower the Pitch of Acoustic Signals in Defense of Territories: A Possible Dishonest Signal of Size?" *Behavioral Ecology* 11, 169–77. Also see Backwell, Patricia, J. Christy, S. Telford, M. Jennions, and N. Passmore (2000), "Dishonest Signaling in a Fiddler Crab," *Proceedings of the Royal Society B: Biological Sciences* 267, 719–24.

5. All collected money was donated to a cancer cause.

6. Taylor, John (1974), "John Doe, Jr.: A Study of His Distribution in Space, Time, and the Social Structure," *Social Forces* 53, 11–21; McFerran, Brent, D. Dahl, G. Fitzsimons, and A. Morales (2009), "I'll Have What She's Having: Effects of Social Influence and Body Type on the Food Choices of Others," *Journal of Consumer Research* 36, 1–15. Fryer, Roland, and Steven Levitt (2002), "Understanding the Black-White Test Score Gap in the First Two Years of School," *National Bureau of Economic Research Paper No. 8975.*

7. White, Katherine, and Darren Dahl (2006), "To Be or Not Be? The Influence of Dissociative Reference Groups on Consumer Preferences," *Journal of Consumer Psychology* 16, 404–14.

8. Hemphill, Cadelle, A. Vanneman, and T. Rahman (2011), "Achievement Gaps: How Hispanic and White Students in Public Schools Perform in Mathematics and Reading on the National Assessment of Educational Progress," U.S. Department of Education, Institute of Education Sciences, National Center for Education Statistics, Washington, DC.

9. For Fordham and Ogbu's original research, see Fordham, Signithia, and John Ogbu (1986), "Black Students' School Successes: Coping with the Burden of 'Acting White,'" *Urban Review* 18, 176–206. For other discussions of acting white, see Carbado, Devon, and Mitu Gulati (2013), *Acting White? Rethinking Race in "Post-Racial" America* (New York: Oxford University Press); and Buck, Stuart (2011), *Acting White: The Ironic Legacy of Desegregation* (New Haven: Yale University Press). Some researchers have even challenged Fordham and Ogbu's conclusions, arguing that both black and white students want to succeed in school and that both show higher levels of self-esteem when they do well. These researchers have suggested that successful students of all races are stigmatized for being geeks or nerds, and so, rather than being about race, the dilemma is about high achievement more broadly. See also Cook, Philip, and Jens Ludwig (1997), "Weighing the Burden of 'Acting White': Are There Race Differences in Attitudes Toward Education?" *Journal of Policy Analysis and Management* 16, 256–78; and Tyson, Karolyn, W. Darity, and D. Castellino (2005), "It's Not 'a Black Thing': Understanding the Burden of Acting White and Other Dilemmas of High Achievement," *American Sociological Review* 70, 582–605.

10. Fryer, Roland, and Paul Torelli (2010), "An Empirical Analysis

of 'Acting White,'" *Journal of Public Economics* 94, 380–96. Also see Bursztyn, Leonardo, and Robert Jensen (2015), "How Does Peer Pressure Affect Educational Investments?" *Quarterly Journal of Economics* 130, 1329-67. Similar effects have been observed for a number of health promotion behaviors. See Oyserman, Daphna, S. Fryberg, and N. Yoder (2007), "Identity-Based Motivation and Health," *Journal of Personality and Social Psychology* 93, 1011–27.

11. Oyserman, Daphna, D. Brickman, D. Bybee, and A. Celious (2006), "Fitting in Matters: Markers of In-group Belonging and Academic Outcomes," *Psychological Science* 17, 854–61.

12. Similar pejorative terms exist for a variety of racial groups: Asian people who dress or act stereotypically white may be called "Twinkies" or "bananas," i.e., yellow on the outside and white on the inside. Adolescent boys who have "baby-faces" or look young are more likely to commit crimes or be involved in delinquent behavior. Just as light-skinned blacks may try harder to shed the label of "acting white," boys who look younger may act tougher to refute the notion that they are childlike. Similarly, some data suggests that Asian-Americans may be more likely to eat fatty traditionally American foods when their American identities are threatened. Guendelman, Maya, S. Cheryan, and B. Monin (2011), "Fitting In but Getting Fat: Identity Threat and Dietary Choices Among U.S. Immigrant Groups," *Psychological Science* 22, 959–67.

13. Executive Office of the President (2013), "Women and Girls in Science, Technology, Engineering, and Math (STEM)," The White House, Washington, DC.

14. Cheryan, Sapna, V. Plaut, P. Davies, and C. Steele (2009), "Ambient Belonging: How Stereotypical Cues Impact Gender Participation in Computer Science," *Journal of Personality and Social Psychology* 97, 1045–60; Cheryan, Sapna, B. Drury, and M. Vichayapai (2012), "Enduring Influence of Stereotypical Computer Science Role Models on Women's Academic Aspirations," *Psychology of Women Quarterly* 37, 72–79; Cheryan, Sapna, A. Meltzoff, and S. Kim (2011), "Classrooms Matter: The Design of Virtual Classrooms Influences Gender Disparities in Computer Science Classes," *Computers & Education* 57, 1825–35.

15. Berger, Jonah, and Morgan Ward (2010), "Subtle Signals of Inconspicuous Consumption," *Journal of Consumer Research* 37, 555–69.

16. Subtle signals are particularly useful when groups want to coordinate without being detected by everyone else. In the 1980s, gay

men needed a way of being out to each other but not to the mainstream. Discrimination was rampant and people could lose their jobs or even face physical abuse for their sexual orientation. So they had to devise subtle signals that could be identified by other gay men but not by outsiders. The "Old Clone" look was one such solution, and included tight jeans, a flannel shirt, construction boots, and a moustache—instantly recognizable by other gay men, but covert enough that most non-gay colleagues would miss the significance.

17. ABC News *Nightline* (2013), "Black Market Counterfeit Goods Rakes in $500 Billion Yearly," *Yahoo! News*; Clifford, Stephanie (2010), "Economic Indicator: Even Cheaper Knockoffs," *New York Times*, July 31, 2010, A1; MarkMonitor, "Seven Best Practices for Fighting Counterfeit Sales Online," MarkMonitor.com White Paper (September 2010).

18. Carvajal, Doreen (2008), "EBay Ordered to Pay $61 Million in Sale of Counterfeit Goods," *New York Times*, July 1, C1, http://www.nytimes.com/2008/07/01/technology/01ebay.html?_r=0.

19. http://money.cnn.com/magazines/fortune/fortune_archive/2005/05/16/8260140/.

20. Raustiala, Kal, and Christopher Sprigman (2006), "The Piracy Paradox: Innovation and Intellectual Property in Fashion Design," *Virginia Law Review* 92, 1687–777.

21. Griffiths, Sarah (2013), "Sorry Popeye, Spinach DOESN'T Make Your Muscles Big: Expert Reveals Sailor's Love of Food Was Due to a Misplaced Decimal," *Daily Mail*, July 3, 1.

22. Berger, Jonah (2008), "Shifting Signals to Help Health: Using Identity Signaling to Reduce Risky Health Behaviors," *Journal of Consumer Research* 35, 509–18.

23. Cheryan, Sapna, V. Plaut, P. Davies, and C. Steele (2009), "Ambient Belonging: How Stereotypical Cues Impact Gender Participation in Computer Science," *Journal of Personality and Social Psychology* 97, 1045–60.

24. In a funny version of identity signaling, a comedian used this strategy to get kids to adopt a new toy. If there is one thing young kids want, it's to not be thought of as babies. They are proud of moving past that stage of their life and see drinking from a bottle and sleeping in a crib as "baby stuff." So a comedian got kids to adopt a toy by telling them it was the only way to prove they were not babies—that if they didn't have the toy, other people would think they still wore diapers.

25. Sean, Young, A. David Nussbaum, and Benoit Monin (2007), "Potential Moral Stigma and Reactions to Sexually Transmitted Diseases: Evidence for a Disjunction Fallacy," *Personality and Social Psychology Bulletin* 33, 789–99.

4. Similar but Different

1. Berger, Jonah, Eric Bradlow, Alex Braunstein, and Yao Zhang (2012), "From Karen to Katie: Using Baby Names to Study Cultural Evolution," *Psychological Science* 23, 1067–73.
2. Bertrand, Marianne, and Sendhil Mullainathan (2004), "Are Emily and Greg More Employable Than Lakisha and Jamal? A Field Experiment on Labor Market Discrimination," *American Economic Review* 94, 991–1013.
3. "Hurricane Katrina Statistics Fast Facts," CNN Library, uploaded August 24, 2015.
4. Landwehr, Jan, A. Labroo, and A. Herrmann (2011), "Gut Liking for the Ordinary: Incorporating Design Fluency Improves Automobile Sales Forecasts," *Marketing Science* 30, 416–29. This effect is stronger among cars that have more complex designs.
5. This text is taken directly from the experimental instructions of Monahan, Jennifer, S. Murphy, and R. Zajonc (2000), "Subliminal Mere Exposure: Specific, General and Diffuse Effects," *Psychological Science* 11, 462–66. See also Gordon, Peter, and Keith Holyoak (1983), "Implicit Learning and Generalization of the 'Mere Exposure' Effect," *Journal of Personality and Social Psychology* 45, 492–500.
6. Novel faces that resemble positively evaluated people are evaluated more positively. See Verosky, Sara, and Alexander Todorov (2010), "Generalization of Affective Learning About Faces to Perceptually Similar Faces," *Psychological Science* 21, 779–85.
7. Bermant, Gordon (1976), *Sexual Behavior: Hard Times with the Coolidge Effect in Psychological Research—The Inside Story*, eds. M. H. Siegel and H. P. Ziegler (New York: Harper and Row).
8. Hirschman, Elizabeth (1980), "Innovativeness, Novelty Seeking and Consumer Creativity," *Journal of Consumer Research* 7, 283–95; Sluckin, Wladyslaw, D. Hargreaves, and A. Colman, "Novelty and Human Aesthetic Preferences," in *Exploration in Animals and Humans*, eds. J. Archer and L. Birke (New York: Van Nostrand Reinhold), 245–69.
9. Aron, Arthur, C. Norman, E. Aron, C. McKenna, and R. Heyman (2000), "Couples' Shared Participation in Novel and Arousing Activities and Experienced Relationship Quality," *Journal of Personality*

and Social Psychology 78, 273–84; Wu, Fang, and Bernardo Huberman (2007), "Novelty and Collective Attention," *Proceedings of the National Academy of Sciences of the United States of America* 104; Buchanan, K. E., and A. Bardi (2010), "Acts of Kindness and Acts of Novelty Affect Life Satisfaction," *Journal of Social Psychology* 150, 235–37. Also see research on the Hawthorne effect.

10. Dewsbury, Donald (1981), "Effects of Novelty on Copulatory Behavior: The Coolidge Effect and Related Phenomena," *Psychological Bulletin* 89, 464–82. This effect is certainly context dependent and has never really been examined in humans.

11. Miller, Claude (1971), "Sexual Satiety in the Male Golden Hamster (Mesocricetus auratus)," doctoral dissertation, University of Georgia, Dissertation Abstracts International 1972: Section A, Humanities and Social Sciences (University Microfilms); and Bunnell, Bradford, B. Boland, and D. Dewsbury (1977), "Copulatory Behavior of Golden Hamsters (Mesocricetus auratus)," *Behaviour* 61, 180–205.

12. For research on Optimum Stimulation Level theory, see Berlyne, Daniel (1960), *Conflict, Arousal, and Curiosity* (New York: McGraw-Hill), 12. Maddi, Salvatore, B. Propst, and I. Feldinger (2006), "Three Expressions of the Need for Variety," *Journal of Personality* 33, 82–98, suggests a U-shaped relationship between stimulation and liking. Too little stimulation is boring and too much is overwhelming, but in between is just right.

13. Colman, Andrew, W. Sluckin, and D. Hargreaves (1981), "The Effect of Familiarity on Preferences for Surnames," *British Journal of Psychology* 72, 363–69.

14. Flavell, John, P. Miller, and S. Miller (1985), *Cognitive Development* (Englewood Cliffs, NJ: Prentice Hall), 101–17; and McCall, Robert, and Paul McGhee (1977), "The Discrepancy Hypothesis of Attention and Affect in Infants," in *The Structuring of Experience*, eds. I. Uzgiris and F. Weizmann (New York: Plenum), 79–210.

15. Simonton, Dean (2006), "Thematic Fame and Melodic Originality in Classical Music: A Multivariate Computer-Content Analysis," *Journal of Personality* 48, 206–19.

16. Uzzi, Brian, S. Mukherjee, M. Stringer, and B. Jones (2013), "Atypical Combinations and Scientific Impact," *Science* 342, 468–72.

17. Chan, Cindy, Jonah Berger, and Leaf Van Boven (2012), "Identifiable but Not Identical: Combining Social Identity and Uniqueness Motives in Choice," *Journal of Consumer Research* 39, 561–73.

18. This study was actually run in 2005, before the advent of most of the online surveys that are popular today. Almost everyone believed the manipulation and some actually expressed sadness that the budgets for academic research were so low.

19. Berger, Michael L. (1980), *The Devil Wagon in God's Country: The Automobile and Social Change in Rural America, 1893–1929* (Hamden, CT: Archon).

20. Rindova, Violina P., and Antoaneta P. Petkova (2007), "When Is a New Thing a Good Thing? The Effects of Technological Change and Product Design on Customer Perceptions of Value Created by Product Innovations," *Organization Science* 18, 217–32; Hargadon, Andrew B., and Yellowlees Douglas (2001), "When Innovations Meet Institutions: Edison and the Design of the Electric Light," *Administrative Science Quarterly* 46, 476–501.

21. These items are often called skeumorphs, or objects that retain design cues or visual aspects from the object on which they are based.

5. Come On Baby, Light My Fire

1. Triplett, Norman (1898), "The Dynamogenic Factors in Pacemaking and Competition," *American Journal of Psychology* 9, 507–33; Strube, Michael (2005), "What Did Triplett Really Find? A Contemporary Analysis of the First Experiment in Social Psychology," *American Journal of Psychology* 118, 271–86; and Brehm, Sharon, S. Kassin, and S. Fein (1999), *Social Psychology* (Boston: Houghton Mifflin).

2. Triplett proposed a number of theories to explain this pattern. Everything from something he called "suction theory" (essentially the aerodynamics that are created by having one rider break the wind) to "encouragement theory" (riding with someone else keeps one's spirits up) to something he called "brain worry theory" (that when people race alone or are leading a race, part of their mind is worried about whether they are going fast enough to win). But the theory he gave the most credence to was something he called "dynamogenic factors": that the presence of another rider aroused the competitive instinct and inspired racers to greater effort.

3. Allport, Floyd (1920), "The Influence of the Group upon Association and Thought," *Journal of Experimental Psychology* 3, 159.

4. Bruce, R. (1941), "An Experimental Analysis of Social Factors Affecting the Performance of White Rats. I. Performance in Learning a Simple Field Situation," *Journal of Comparative Psychology* 31,

363–77; Simmel, Edward (1962), "Social Facilitation of Exploratory Behavior in Rats," *Journal of Comparative and Physiological Psychology* 5, 831–33; Stamm, John (1961), "Social Facilitation in Monkeys," *Psychological Reports* 8, 479–84; Scott, John, and C. McCray (1967), "Allelomimetic Behavior in Dogs: Negative Effects of Competition on Social Facilitation," *Journal of Comparative and Physiological Psychology* 63, 316–19; Chen, Shisan (1937), "Social Modification of the Activity of Ants in Nest-Building," *Physiological Zoology* 10, 420–36; and Bayer, E. (1929), "Beitrage zur Zweikomponentheorie des Hungers," *Zeitschrift für Psychologie* 112, 1–S4.

5. Pessin, Joseph (1933), "The Comparative Effects of Social and Mechanical Stimulation on Memorizing," *American Journal of Psychology,* 45, 263–70; Pessin, Joseph, and Richard Husband (1933), "Effects of Social Stimulation on Human Maze Learning," *Journal of Abnormal and Social Psychology* 28, 148–54; and Rosenbloom, Tova, S. Amit, A. Perlman, D. Estreich, and E. Kirzner (2007), "Success on a Practical Driver's License Test with and Without the Presence of Another Testee," *Accident Analysis & Prevention* 39, 1296–301.

6. Klopfer, Peter (1958), "Influence of Social Interaction on Learning Rates in Birds," *Science* 128, 903–4; Alee, W., and R. Masure (1936), "A Comparison of Maze Behavior in Paired and Isolated Shell Parakeets (Melopsittacus undulatus Shaw)," *Journal of Comparative Psychology* 22, 131–55.

7. Fox, Margalit (2008), "Robert Zajonc, Who Looked at Mind's Ties to Actions, Is Dead at 85," *New York Times,* A42; Gorlick, Adam (2008), "Robert Zajonc, Pioneer of Social Psychology, Dies at 85, *Stanford News*, December 11, http://news.stanford.edu/news/2009/january7/zajobit-010709.html; Burnstein, Eugene (2009), "Robert B. Zajonc (1923–2008)," *American Psychologist* 64, 558–59.

8. Zajonc, Robert, A. Heingart, and E. Herman (1969), "Social Enhancement and Impairment of Performance in the Cockroach," *Journal of Personality and Social Psychology* 13, 83. For a review, see Zajonc, Robert, "Social Facilitation," *Science* 149, 269–74.

9. Markus, Hazel (1978), "The Effect of Mere Presence on Social Facilitation: An Unobtrusive Test," *Journal of Experimental Social Psychology* 14, 389–97.

10. Michaels, J. W., J. M. Blommel, R. M. Brocato, R. A. Linkous, and J. S. Rowe (1982). "Social Facilitation and Inhibition in a Natural Setting," *Replications in Social Psychology* 2, 21–24.

11. To this day, there are still competing theories about what drives social facilitation. Some, like Zajonc's major theoretical advance in 1965, focus on drives. The presence of others acts as a source of arousal, or activation, which enhances the emission of a dominant response. For well-learned tasks, that dominant response is correct, so we do better. Michaels, J. W, J. M. Blommel, R. M. Brocato, R. A. Linkous, and J. S. Rowe (1982), "Social Facilitation and Inhibition in a Natural Setting," *Replications in Social Psychology* 2, 21–24.

12. Social facilitation can also happen when people feel like others are present (i.e., in the presence of a picture of someone), even if no one else is physically there.

13. Cudy, Amy, K. Doherty, and M. Bos (2010), "OPOWER: Increasing Energy Efficiency Through Normative Influence (A)," *Harvard Business School Case 911–016*.

14. Nolan, Jessica, P. Schultz, R. Cialdini, N. Goldstein, and V. Griskevicius (2008), "Normative Social Influence Is Underdetected," *Personality and Social Psychology Bulletin* 7, 913–23; Cialdini, Robert, and Wesley Schultz (2004), "Understanding and Motivating Energy Conservation via Social Norms," report submitted to the William and Flora Hewlett Foundation, 1–6.

15. Allcott, Hunt (2011), "Social norms and energy conservation," *Journal of Public Economics* 95, 1082–95.

16. "Opower Utility Partners Save Six Terawatt-Hours of Energy, over $700 Million for Consumers," Opower press release, Jannuary 14, 2015, https://opower.com/company/news-press/press_releases/114.

17. Berger, Jonah, and Devin Pope (2011), "Can Losing Lead to Winning?" *Management Science* 57, 817–27. That losing leads to winning is particularly noteworthy here, given the stakes. NBA players get paid to play basketball. And while they don't get paid for each game they win, like most jobs, over the course of their careers, they get paid based on performance. The more their teams win, the more they ultimately get paid. Yet, even with all these millions at stake, losing still leads to winning.

18. This problem was adapted from Heath, Chip, Richard Larrick, and George Wu (1999), "Goals as Reference Points," *Cognitive Psychology* 38, 79–109.

19. Notably, round numbers often serve as salient reference points, motivating people to work hard until they achieve them. High school students, for example, are more likely to retake the SAT if they score just below, rather than just above, a round number.

Students who score a 990, for instance, are much more likely to retake the test than people who score 1000, even though the scores are almost the same. See Pope, Devin, and Uri Simonsohn (2011), "Round Numbers as Goals Evidence from Baseball, SAT Takers and the Lab," *Psychological Science* 22, 71–78.

20. Page, Lionel (2009), "The Momentum Effect in Competitions: Field Evidence from Tennis Matches," Econometric Society Australasian Meeting, Australian National University, Canberra, July 7–10, 2009 (unpublished).

21. Kivetz, Ran, O. Urminsky, and Y. Zheng (2006), "The Goal-Gradient Hypothesis Resurrected: Purchase Acceleration, Illusionary Goal Progress, and Customer Retention," *Journal of Marketing Research* 43, 39–58.

22. Brown, Judson (1948), "Gradients of Approach and Avoidance Responses and Their Relation to Level of Motivation," *Journal of Comparative and Physiological Psychology* 41, 450–65; Hull, Clark L. (1932), "The Goal-Gradient Hypothesis and Maze Learning," *Psychological Review* 39, 25–43; and Hull, C., (1934), "The Rats' Speed of Locomotion Gradient in the Approach to Food," *Journal of Comparative Psychology* 17, 393–422.

23. Fershtman, C., and U. Gneezy (2011), "The Trade-off between Performance and Quitting in High-Power Tournaments," *Journal of the European Economic Association* 9, 318–36. Quitting is particularly likely when direct comparison is facilitated. When competitors can easily see how they are doing relative to one another, that should increase the chance that people who are slightly behind will get motivated, but also that people who are far behind recognize their position and give up.

24. Tuckfield, Bradford, D. Berkeley, K. Milkman, and M. Schweitzer, "Quitting: The Downside of Great Expectations in Competitions," Wharton School Working Paper (under revision).

25. Rogers, Todd, and Don Moore (2014), "The Motivating Power of Under-Confidence: 'The Race Is Close but We're Losing,'" *HKS Working Paper No. RWP14-047.*

26. Irwin, Neil (2015), "Why a Presidential Campaign Is the Ultimate Start-up," *New York Times,* June 4, BU1.

Conclusion: Putting Social Influence to Work

1. There is a huge literature on neighborhood effects. For some recent reviews, see Leventhal, Tama, and Jeanne Brooks-Gunn (2000), "The Neighborhoods They Live In: The Effects of

Neighborhood Residence on Child and Adolescent Outcomes," *Psychological Bulletin* 126, 309–37; and Sampson, Robert, K. Morenoff, and T. Gannon-Rowley (2002), "'Assessing Neighborhood Effects': Social Processes and New Directions in Research," *Annual Review of Sociology*, 443–78.

2. The answer, of course, is not an either-or. Genetics and family factors may predispose people to have certain challenges that neighborhoods then exacerbate. Lower-income families may be less able to pay for kids' ADHD medicine, and local schools may be less equipped to give such children the necessary personal attention. Similarly, resources allow people to overcome challenges as they arise. Higher-income areas not only have better schools, but parents can more easily pay for tutoring if their kids aren't doing well.

3. Kling, Jeffrey, J. Liebman, and L. Katz (2007), "Experimental Analysis of Neighborhood Effects," *Econometrica* 75, 83–119; Ludwig, Jens, G. Duncan, L. Gennetian, L. Katz, R. Kessler, J. Kling, and L. Sanbonmatsu (2013), "Long-Term Neighborhood Effects on Low-Income Families: Evidence from Moving to Opportunity," *National Bureau of Economic Research Working Paper No. 18772*; Katz, Lawrence, J. Kling, J. Liebman (2000), "Moving to Opportunity in Boston: Early Result of a Randomized Mobility Experiment," *National Bureau of Economic Research Working Paper Number 7973*; Ludwig, Jens, G. Duncan, L. Gennetian, L. Katz, R. Kessler, J. Kling, and L. Sanbonmatsu (2012), "Neighborhood Effects on the Long-term Well-being of Low-Income Adults," *Science* 337, 1505–10.

4. Chetty, Raj, N. Hendren, and L. Katz (2015), "The Effects of Exposure to Better Neighborhoods on Children: New Evidence from the Moving to Opportunity Experiment," *National Bureau of Economic Research Working Paper Number 21156*; Chetty, Raj, and Nathaniel Hendren (2015), "The Impacts of Neighborhoods on Intergenerational Mobility: Childhood Exposure Effects and County-Level Estimates," working paper.

5. The positive effect of moving on income holds even when accounting for the disruptive impact that moving can have on a child's life. In fact, the disruption may be one reason that Moving to Opportunity has a slightly negative effect on children who were older when their families moved. Not only was there less time to soak up the beneficial effects of the new neighborhood, moving disrupted the strong roots that people had already created.

Index